Break Free from Toxic
Relationships and Patterns,
Set Healthy Boundaries,
Claim Independence

Dylan Walker

CONQUERING CODEPENDENCY FOREVER WITH *Emotional Regulation*

YOUR FREE GIFT

As a way of saying thanks for your purchase, I'm offering the book Overcoming Limiting Beliefs for FREE to my readers.
To get instant access just go to:

https://dylanwalkerbooks.com/selflove-free-bonus

Inside the book, you will discover:

- **10 steps to break through your limiting beliefs**: Even if you struggled with negative thinking before, this book will be the change you need.
- **An action plan to end sabotaging yourself**: Learn exactly how to reframe your thoughts with just 10-minutes a day.
- **Reduce stress and achieve unshakable confidence**: A healthy mindset leads to achieving your goals and dreams. It's time to take back your life!

If you want to stop negative thinking and start making progress towards your dreams make sure to grab the free book.

TABLE OF CONTENTS

PART 2: OVERCOME! EMOTIONAL REGULATION STRATEGY

PART 3: STAYING FREE

INTRODUCTION

Codependency is a lie that codependents tell themselves.

> *"The lie about co-dependency is that your partner needs you as much as you need [them]. In reality, [they] can usually replace you much more easily than you can replace [them]."*
>
> **(GUNTHER ET AL., 2020)**

Let's face it. We all lie at some point to someone but some of the biggest lies we tell are those that we tell ourselves. These lies cause us to live in denial of the reality of our lives. This is why such lies can often be the most destructive forces that exist. We often delude ourselves into thinking that when we love someone beyond fathom, the other person reciprocates. We may even delude ourselves into thinking that such an emotion is healthy and sustainable in the long run—a forever kind of love that we have always dreamed of.

However, this cannot be further from the truth. If you have ever found yourself enough in love that you would take a bullet for someone—heck, you'd even take two—then you probably know exactly what I am talking about. Given enough time, you would have probably realized that you loved them way more than they loved you. Although this kind of epiphany is often heartbreaking, you should thank your stars that you came to that realization.

Many codependents go their entire lives without even realizing that they are part of the toxic cycle that has seeped into their lives. They keep searching for the perfect love to come along to complete their broken selves. Practically, that is not how any of this works. In reality, we are responsible for healing and mending our broken selves before we can have a healthy relationship. This also includes completing ourselves before we seek a companion. Two broken and incomplete people cannot complete each other. Rumi, the mystical 13th-century scholar and poet, cleverly stated,

> *"Never give from the depths of your well, but from your overflow."*
>
> **(T. C. M. World, 2020)**

If you have struggled with feelings of being incomplete, broken, or unhealed, and have ever felt that you need a partner to help fix you, then it is likely that you have struggled with codependency in your relationships. This book can help you overcome it. How do I know this? I know this because I have been there, and done that. I've been studying the best methods for overcoming dependency and avoiding relapses for at least five years now. I am deeply invested in helping you achieve the same freedom from being a love addict myself. I've become better at sustaining healthy relationships, without exceptions.

I understand how difficult it might seem to be able to find freedom from toxic relationship cycles and can show you how to work things out without stress. I love helping people overcome issues with their relationships, particularly those pertaining to codependency and people-pleasing problems. I'm confident that the strategies I share with you here will help you immensely.

Whether you display codependent tendencies sometimes, but are unsure if you are codependent or not, in a toxic relationship due to your codependent tendencies and finding it hard to set and maintain healthy boundaries to claim your independence, or are a people-pleaser who always says yes to your detriment, this book will help guide you. I can promise you that this will prove a valuable resource on codependency that will help you identify if you have codependent tendencies and their impact on your life and relationships. It will act as a comprehensive guide on what codependency means, what codependent traits are, how to break free from toxic relationships, how to set healthy boundaries, and how to claim your independence. You will learn about emotional regulation and how to build it, how to put an end to people-pleasing, and how to put yourself first when it matters most.

This book is divided into three parts. The first part focuses on the dynamics of a codependent relationship, the enablers, and who codependents attract and are attracted to.

The second part expressly discusses prioritizing oneself, why narcissists are drawn to codependents, overcoming fear of abandonment, letting go of toxic relationships, building self-worth and self-confidence, and utilizing emotional regulation as a tool against toxic relationships.

The third and final part of the book covers why and how to keep boundaries, and how to transition from codependent relationships to healthier interdependent relationships. This is a self-help workbook that can help you discover how to love yourself, forgive yourself, master your emotions, stop toxic thinking patterns, thoughts, and emotions, overcome negativity and build your self-confidence to achieve inner happiness and success. So, keep reading if you are ready to rediscover a new you that is healed and free from codependent binds.

PART 1:

THE ROOTS OF CODEPENDENCY

CHAPTER 1: TRAPPED IN CODEPENDENCY

Every romantic relationship and many platonic friendships head off with a great start. We often like to explore new interests and experiences with our newfound friends or lovers. All romantic relationships start with a honeymoon stage, where the couple tends to be inseparable and seem to gravitate toward each other like magnets if you observe their body language closely enough. It is also possible in some romantic relationships that one partner may be more fond of PDA (public displays of affection) or be clingier than the other. However, this initial phase—where new friends or lovers experience the excitement in the relationship—is not to be confused with codependency. Codependency is far more sinister in terms of its power imbalance and relationship dynamic.

What a Codependent Relationship Looks Like

A codependent relationship is one where there is a lopsided power dynamic between two people, one of whom is a love addict aka codependent and the other is a love avoidant aka enabler. The codependent is addicted to the avoidant, and the avoidant is usually addicted to some or the other bad habit that the codependent wants to save them from. To do this, the codependent will shower all their love and affection on the enabler, hoping the enabler would somehow, someday wake up from their moral slumber at the touch of their proverbial true love's kiss.

However, the enabler thrives on the need to be doted on and never really accomplishes this goal while the codependent goes on sacrificing themselves, their time, their money, and their emotional energy into this relationship until they reach a breaking point where they are filled with resentment and grief at the thought that they haven't been able to "rescue" their partner from themselves.

At the end of the day, they realize that this is a one-sided relationship. They experience high levels of anxiety because of having to constantly fulfill their partner's need to be happy, not realizing that no matter what you do for someone else, you can never, truly, keep them completely happy all the time. It is interesting to note that codependents, even outside of their relationships, struggle with anxiety, and channeling it towards their enabling partner—rather than sitting with their feelings—seems to be a coping mechanism for them. They have extreme people-pleasing tendencies that cause them to constantly make sacrifices, even if it is to their detriment. Codependent relationships also lack the healthy boundaries and structure that exist in normal healthy relationships.

However, if codependents do not realize their role in this—that you cannot save anyone from themselves, that you can only do so much for a person, and that change has to come from within—they can find the same patterns repeating in all their relationships until they learn how to form healthy relationships.

Still unsure if you are codependent?

If you want to figure out whether you are in a codependent relationship, ask yourself the following questions:

1. Do you feel like your true happiness lies in doing things for the other person to the extent that you find no happiness or satisfaction in doing other things in life?
2. Do you feel like you would do anything to keep the other person happy, despite the cost to yourself?
3. Do you feel an emotional need or compulsion to stay in the relationship even if you are fully aware of your partner hurting you or your well-being?
4. Does the thought of putting your own needs first make you feel guilty to the point that you have never expressed your needs or personal desires to the other person?
5. Do you find yourself ending up using all your time, energy, and other resources (if applicable) to provide everything your partner asks you for?
6. Do you/have you ever/are you willing to ignore your own morals or conscience to do what your partner wants?
7. Do you feel you are always anxious about your relationship with your partner because you are always trying to make them happy?
8. Do you find yourself constantly worrying about what you may do to disappoint them, resulting in them abandoning you?
9. Do you feel the need to change your partner to help them become a better person or save them from themselves?
10. Do you feel uncomfortable spending time alone and feel like a part of you is incomplete or missing?

If you have answered *yes* to at least five of the above questions, then you are likely codependent. A codependent person will experience an extreme internal emotional battle about separating themselves from their enabler since their sense of well-being is completely based on sacrificing their needs for their partner. However, the good news is that since you are reading this, you are already on a path of recovery.

The Parties Involved and Their Roles

Codependents are usually born and forged into what they are as a result of dysfunctional families. A dysfunctional family is usually run by a narcissistic—or just plain toxic—parent. The other family members, especially children, take on different roles depending on their situations and keep cycling these roles as the family dynamic shifts over the years. It is to be noted that not all dysfunctional families have all the roles going on at a time, but all of them have at least one at any given point.

The Taker

The Taker is also known as the Golden Child of the family. This role pops up in the family if one or both parents have a narcissistic personality disorder. The parent will favor the golden child above everyone else, but not for their inherent qualities. Rather, it is because the narcissistic parent(s) see themselves in the golden child. The golden child is a personification of the parents' admiration of themselves and not for the child so their love is completely conditional on the golden child meeting their standards and fulfilling all their demands. Nothing that the golden child does can ever be wrong and they get to have the biggest slice of the pie in the family, whether it be material benefits that the parents provide for their children or anything else. All demands of the golden child are met as long as the golden child is compliant. This is why the golden child is called a taker. Usually, the taker grows up to develop avoidant attachments and becomes the enabler for the codependents because takers thrive on the need to be doted on and are used to having their every need met.

The Caretaker

The Caretaker's role in a dysfunctional family is to care for everyone. The caretaker usually ends up taking on this role because of parental neglect towards the children so the caretaker becomes the proxy parent for themselves and their siblings if any—and sometimes the parents if they are into self-sabotaging and self-destructive habits.

However, just because they take on the parent's role, does not mean that they can provide it. They usually end up in damage control roles which means making breakfast for the siblings if the parent has not returned from their night out or pacifying their siblings *after* the parent has finished their venting and is done with all the abuses. The caretaker usually facilitates the harm in the hope of trying to keep the peace and silence or deny any voice that tries to seek accountability for the family dysfunction.

Caretakers usually go on to become codependents and may seek the same qualities in their partner as they have observed in their parents. For example, if their parents were alcoholics, they may be attracted to someone with an alcohol addiction or a history of alcohol abuse.

The Addict

The Addict—also known as the Identified Patient—is the living, breathing personification of all the core issues of the dysfunctional family. This person develops an addiction—be it substance abuse, gambling, sex, or gaming—and the entire family finds themselves gathering under one banner to help the addict out of their addiction and save them through any means possible, healthy or otherwise. This serves as a distraction for the other family members to focus on, instead of the actual dysfunction prevalent in their family. Interestingly, the addict develops the addiction as a result of the family dysfunction in the first place. So the addict usually continues to relapse despite all the "help" offered because:

- They feel annoyed or frustrated that they are the ones being focused on and being helped because they know, deep down, that the core issue of their family is something else entirely.
- They may subconsciously realize that their family only acts relatively close to anything normal and functions as one unit if they are in their "addiction phase".
- It also lets both their family and themselves live in denial of the deeper, more troubling, core issues that they may not be ready to face head-on.

The addict may also relapse into their addiction in times of distress or if they are triggered by something in their romantic relationship, especially if it is an unhealthy one.

The Hero

The Hero is that child who substitutes for the lack of an emotionally available parent by becoming the ultra-efficient high-achiever with a savior complex. They are usually ready to take on any issues that arise in the household. They tend to go on to become workaholics because not only are they used to being high-functioning individuals, but also their professional accomplishments help to fill the gap in their lives resulting from being emotionally insecure.

They may also go on to seek romantic partners who are emotionally unavailable and subconsciously recreate the dynamics that played out in their family when they were growing up. Because of this, many heroes can end up being depressed, chronically stressed, anxious, fatigued, or burned out.

The Scapegoat

The Scapegoat is the proverbial blame vessel for everything that goes wrong in the dysfunctional family. Whether it is their fault or not is immaterial. Scapegoats are often aware of their role in the family—that they are being blamed unfairly and will continue being blamed probably forever. This may make them feel lonely, abandoned, and unloved. They are also usually the only ones who can be honest about the real underlying issues in their family—that others are in denial or blind to—and may often call out the family for it. For this, they get appointed to their role of scapegoat.

The scapegoat may also be chosen due to other criteria which may or may not make any sense to a normal person such as being chronically ill or physically weaker, being academically weaker or having learning disabilities, being socially awkward, or simply having a slightly different appearance than the rest of the siblings. In families run by a narcissistic parent, the scapegoat is often pitted against the golden child, by the parent, as a distraction from the core family issues. Scapegoats may often grow up developing self-sabotaging tendencies and experience difficulty forming and sustaining healthy connections with others.

The Mascot

The Mascot's role is a self-appointed one. This is the proverbial clown of the family who attempts to diffuse any tensions through humor and fun. However, the catch with this dysfunctional role is that while they are good at diffusing an impending disaster, they always feel immense pressure to put on their show the next time they see the storm clouds gathering. They may go on to become codependents because they always go the extra mile for those whom they care for, even at their own expense. Mascots are also prone to depression and anxiety because of their high-stakes role in their dysfunctional family.

The Lost Child

The Lost Child is the family loner whom no one ever notices and who doesn't make an effort to get noticed either. The lost child operates from a place of fear and thus blends in, scared to draw attention to themselves, especially in an abusive family. Despite their dislike of attention, they may feel ignored or neglected, yet struggle to form meaningful relationships as an adult because they are hardwired to equate being ignored with being safe. Although they appear quiet on the outside they may have intense emotions and may also struggle with overthinking.

Not a Virtue!—Codependency Isn't Equal to Selflessness, Patience, or Forbearance

A lot of people who read about codependency including codependents themselves—see their attachment style as some sort of virtue, be it selflessness, patience, or forbearance. The fact that they may never have seen these values modeled to them in healthy relationships certainly does not help. Since they do not know what these virtues look like when embodied by emotionally healthy people, they confuse the extremes that are observed in codependency to be virtues of love. However, it is important to understand that anything that enables bad behavior cannot be a virtue. If you are expecting your partner to come around and give up their addiction or any other "bad" behavior that you may have a problem with, simply because they are moved by the love you have given them or the sacrifices you have made for them, then ask yourself: Would you give up eating junk food if you knew you would earn $50 every time you ate it? Enabling works the same way. While it is important to love someone unconditionally, it is also important to let them know that certain behaviors are wrong. It is important to set boundaries and consequences for your romantic partners and let them know that certain behaviors will not be tolerated. Without this crucial aspect, relationships can easily turn toxic and abusive in no time. It is no wonder that the codependent person ends up feeling used and abused. After all, they let it happen. It is very important for them—and everyone else—to realize this harsh truth.

Selflessness must not come at the cost of your own well-being. You can only give from what you have. It is important to make sure you are happy to share a slice of your joy with others. Patience and forbearance are best practiced when you are facing an internal conflict of intense emotions, and not when you are being blatantly abused and taken advantage of by someone else. That is not patience; that is enabling.

Patience in the face of all the bricks and lemons that life throws at you is one thing. In the face of abusive behavior that your partner displays towards you, it is another.

Forbearance, when you are experiencing mourning, grief, loss, despair, intense anger, vindictiveness, jealousy, and envy, is one thing. When you are experiencing physical, verbal, or emotional abuse from your partner, it is another.

How a Codependent Relationship Begins

A codependent relationship can almost always be traced back to both parties' dysfunctional childhood experiences. Healthy relationships are all about give and take, where each partner flip-flops between the roles of the cherished one and the nurturer. However, in a codependent relationship, one partner is always stuck in the role of a nurturer while the other is always being nurtured. This can take a toll on the mental health of the caretaker who is always giving to the relationship without receiving anything in return. One may ask, why would anyone do something like this to themselves? The answer lies in their behavioral patterns learned from their dysfunctional family dynamics during their childhood. These behaviors that they learned as children that helped them survive the dysfunction go on to become unhealthy and problematic when forming adult relationships. Codependency is a learned coping mechanism for mainly two kinds of parenting: overprotective and under-protective.

Overprotective Parents

Overprotective or "helicopter parents" tend to be over-involved in their children's lives. They will intervene in any and every issue the child may face in their lives and solve it for them on their behalf. Because of this, the child never faces rejection or hurt. On the flip side, the parents may also treat the child like a friend and over-involve the child in their own lives, over-sharing about their financial or relationship issues. Because of this, the child loses their sense of self and feels guilty about seeking independence outside of the parent-child dynamic.

Under-Protective Parents

Under-protective or negligent parents, as the name suggests, are simply too uninvolved to ensure their child's emotional growth. Their reasons could be many—from being caught up at work, battling addiction or mental health issues, to just being completely chilled out about the whole parenting deal. Whatever the cause, the result is a child who has grown up too fast for their own good to compensate for their parent's glaring absence. They have taken on parenting roles like taking care of their siblings, working extra jobs, or managing the home on behalf of the parent. Such children go on to become too independent and struggle to form healthy relationships because they cannot accept emotional support.

Why It's Difficult to Get Out

Codependency is a learned behavior. The good news is it can be unlearned as well but this is easier said than done, for the following reasons:

- You have no clue.
- You have happy memories too.
- Your partner is also codependent.
- Your happiness depends on them, literally.
- You're obsessed.
- Everyone else seems to be okay with it.
- You have internalized shame.

You Have No Clue

One of the major reasons why individuals struggle to break free of codependent relationships is because they simply have no clue that they are in one. When you recreate dysfunctional patterns that you have been following since your childhood, you are only doing what you perceive is normal. Even if you are not happy with it, you will not seek to change it because it is within your comfort zone.

You Have Happy Memories Too

Another reason why codependents struggle to break free is because of the confusing hot and cold nature of the relationship. Every relationship has moments of happiness including codependent ones. Some enablers and addicts may promise their codependent partners that they will change before relapsing into their old habits. This game of will-they-won't-they becomes a source of hope for the codependents who invest their energy in the "potential" they see in their relationship. In such scenarios, the question codependents should ask themselves is, *How much worse does it need to get?*

Your Partner Is Also Codependent

Having a codependent partner is also a major reason why people struggle to let go of such unhealthy relationships or even set healthy boundaries in the existing one. The partner also has a hard time letting go and constantly breaks boundaries to pull you back in or pursue you. While this is not very emotionally healthy for either of the parties involved, it could be flattering to feel wanted and pursued, and thus, the couple can slip into their old patterns.

Your Happiness Depends on Them, Literally

One of the foundational traits of a codependent relationship is that your happiness literally depends on your partner. You build your entire identity and sense of self around them. You need them to validate you, barring which you begin to feel worthless and unlovable.

You're Obsessed

While most codependents are highly intuitive about other people's emotions and needs, they tend to get quite carried away when they form relationships, to the point that they can obsess over their partner's needs and interests, thereby neglecting their own in the process. When you plan and build your entire life around someone else, it becomes difficult to untwine yourself and think of yourself as a separate entity.

Everyone Else Seems to Be Okay with It

Another very common factor in so many cultures as to why codependents continue to stay on in their toxic relationship is that everyone around them seems to be completely alright with it. They may find their family, friends, or close social circles telling them how their relationship is picture-perfect and how good they are together. Since they are convinced that what they are doing is both morally and socially acceptable, they might feel that it is unacceptable to break away, even when the relationship progresses from bad to worse.

Internalized Shame

Many a time, the codependents' sense of shame that they are not worthy of "proper" love and affection could play a major role in having them stick around in toxic relationships. They may feel that they deserve to be treated as they are. Alternatively, they may be repeating the family dysfunction of "not airing your dirty laundry in public" and may feel ashamed of talking about the abuse to their peers or seeking any other sort of help. Thus, maintaining the status quo and the illusion of having a perfect life becomes the utmost priority.

Why It's Unhealthy to Continue in Codependency

Although codependency in a romantic relationship may start off as any normal relationship does—with the honeymoon phase, stomach butterflies, and fluttering hearts, where neither can keep their eyes or hands off the other—it can soon rear its ugly head and become toxic very fast. That is because a codependent relationship normally takes place between two kinds of individuals: a Taker and a Giver. The taker—also usually the one with the "bigger problems"—insatiably needs love and attention to be happy. This person will drain the energy out of their partner because nothing that their partner does for them can ever be enough. The giver obsessively takes care of the taker, exhausting all their energy and resources, even if it comes at the cost of their own happiness. This often leads the giver to make self-sabotaging and self-destructive decisions to please their partner.

Staying in a codependent relationship is not just unhealthy for the giver, but also the taker. Takers play the will-they-won't-they game when it comes to their issues. Every time they see the giver losing hope, they show signs of improvement to retain their partner but eventually relapse into their old habits because they know that they won't be facing any true consequences in their relationship. This lack of seriousness to improve their situation can cause their issues to escalate and eventually backfire for good, as they face the consequences in situations where people would not tolerate their behavior. As for the giver, the confusion created by the selfishness and manipulative behavior of their partner may cause them to develop mental health issues like depression, chronic anxiety, stress, and fatigue. They may also end up depleting their other resources, like physical health or financial assets, in repeated attempts to play savior to the taker.

Codependency FAQs

Who Is Most Affected by Codependency?

In terms of gender, both men and women are equally prone to codependency. Individuals who are in a relationship with someone who has an addiction or mental health issue seem to be at a higher risk. Children who grow up with abusive or excessively demanding parents are prone to develop codependent traits.

Can a Codependent Have Healthy Relationships?

With therapy and inner healing, yes! But in their codependent state, unfortunately, no.

Is Codependency Treatable?

Yes, codependency is a mental health issue that can improve if a person is willing to resolve their traumas with some form of therapy, be it self-therapy, group therapy, or by seeking professional help.

CHAPTER 2: THE PSYCHOLOGY AND ENABLERS OF CODEPENDENCY

Previously, we learned the basics of codependency, its causes, and the harm it can cause to all the parties involved. Now let us delve deep into how the brain of a codependent individual works, the attachment styles that enable codependency, the cycle of narcissism and codependency, and the infamous connection between empaths and codependents. After that, we'll move on to seeking solutions.

How Do Codependents Think?

Codependency is a trauma response. This trauma can be generational or experienced and is usually a result of being constantly abused by people who claim to love you, being berated in the form of negative labels like *worthless*, *unlovable*, *unwanted*, etc., being blamed unfairly, having yourself or your feelings invalidated, having been subjected to unreliable and confusing parenting patterns, having your boundaries violated, not receiving appropriate guidance from caregivers, and feeling constantly anxious, scared or restless as a child, due to parents or caregivers neglecting your emotional or physical needs. This trauma that codependents usually experience early in life can lead to negative thinking patterns that, although inaccurate, can turn into self-fulfilling prophecies as codependents subconsciously seek out partners with whom they can potentially recreate the trauma and dysfunction.

The following questionnaire can help you unpack your codependent thinking patterns:

1. Do you feel that every wrong thing that happens to those you care about is your fault somehow?
2. Do you feel worthless—as if you do not deserve to be loved, unless you are helping someone you love, in some way?
3. Do you feel a need to be perfect—like you have no room for any error or mistake in your life—or at least paint the picture of being such?
4. Do you feel guilty every time you focus on your needs and spend any of your own money or time on yourself?
5. Do you feel responsible for someone else's happiness?
6. Do you find anger to be something that you should be afraid of?
7. Do you feel like you are valuable only when someone else tells you that you are?
8. Do you find it difficult to delegate work to others and that you just cannot trust anyone else to do a good job of it?
9. Do you feel overwhelmed by your own emotions and unsure of what to do with them?

10. Do you think that there is only one proper way to do things and that any other way is simply wrong or abhorrent?
11. Do you feel responsible for other people's emotions, and especially for their happiness?
12. Do you feel that you need to prove your value by working doubly hard, taking care of others more than they take care of you, giving up something you value, and never making a mistake while you're at it?
13. Do you think that things will start to fall apart if you do not volunteer to take responsibility and get things under control?
14. Do you feel the need to save people from themselves for their own good and that if left alone, they will mess up?
15. Do you think that if everyone would just follow your advice or at least let you help them out, their lives would be a lot better?

If you have answered "Yes" to at least 10 of the above questions, you likely have codependent thinking patterns. However, having codependent thinking patterns does not mean that you will end up being a slave to codependency. You can unlearn these thinking patterns with positive self-talk and affirmations. How you talk to yourself is very important. Challenge your negative beliefs about yourself and don't let your inner voice tell you that you are unlovable or unworthy. Learning to say "No" to your negative inner voice first can pave the way for you to say "No" to others who drain your energy, as well.

What Enables Codependency?

Although codependent relationships are most common in romantic settings, they are also prevalent in family settings. Let's explore the different circumstances that help this unhealthy mindset thrive.

Codependency in a Family Setting

A parent can be codependent on the child and take on the role of a caretaker. While the child is struggling with their "problems" the parent continues to enable their misdemeanors by ensuring that they never face any serious consequences for them or by acting as a "shield" and absorbing the worst impact of the said consequences even if they occur. It could happen with parents who are struggling with an addict in the family or a child with other mental issues. They may center their lives around "helping" the child out because they believe that the child cannot survive without them. They may go to the extent of bailing them out of jail repeatedly, making food for them, cleaning up their house after them, paying their utility bills, and even paying them an allowance despite knowing that it would end up getting spent on drugs.

Despite the parent showing disappointment in their child's behavior time and again, they continue to enable their child's dysfunction by refusing to let their child take responsibility. They also need to feel needed by someone and in this case, their child's need, even if it is for all the wrong reasons, acts as a source of fulfillment for their self-worth.

Codependency in a Romantic Setting

Most of the ways that romantic codependent partners enable their partners' issues are under the pretext of unconditional love. They may make excuses for themselves for their unhealthy enabling of their partner's dysfunction by telling themselves that since they love their partner, they should be willing to do anything for them. Or they may tell themselves that this is the only way they know to love and live—that they have been doing this for so long that they don't know what else to do.

They may also operate from a sense of subconscious fear for their partner's well-being—afraid that their partner cannot survive if they are not around to guide and save their partner from themselves and fix their messes afterward. Because of this, they may feel a need to control a situation that they feel is heading toward a downward spiral. They may exert this control over their partner's life by taking responsibility for their partner's finances, personal and legal affairs, etc., allowing their partner to use their resources without their permission and putting their own needs on the back burner. Alternatively, they simply rush in and sweep their partner's mistakes under the rug to prevent them from facing consequences.

The Attachment Styles That Enable Codependency

The attachment style that most correlates to codependent behaviors is the anxious attachment style. People who have an anxious attachment style tend to display all the characteristics of a codependent partner. They often prioritize their own needs below their partner's, feel the urge to stay close to their partner, enmesh their emotions with that of their partner and let them affect their own emotional state. They base their sense of happiness, fulfillment, and self-worth upon how much they are keeping their partner happy and end up feeling worthless if any of these goals are not achieved, even if they are not to blame for the non-fulfillment.

The taker or the addict, on the other hand, usually displays a dismissive-avoidant or fearful-avoidant (anxious-avoidant) attachment style. They may withdraw from their partners when the going gets tough or when they are required to display openness and vulnerability in the relationship, and (as much as the partner demands closeness) push their partner away. They may also respond to any kind of conflict, or issue within the relationship, by pulling away from the relationship.

The dismissive-avoidant attachment usually correlates to the role of the addict. Such individuals may be addicted to something outside their relationship, be it work, gaming, gambling, or substances. They derive their sense of self-worth from these addictions. To escape their codependent patterns, they may need to extricate their sense of fulfillment from their work or other addictions to experience a healthy relationship.

The fearful-avoidant, on the other hand, can take on the role of both a caretaker and an enabler and keep alternating between these two. This is because fearful-avoidants have a subconscious desire to feel wanted but withdraw from relationships if the connection between them and their partner becomes too close for comfort. They may swoop in to act as saviors when their partner needs them, but withdraw when they are offered help in return. Because of their emotional misalignment and internal conflict, they may exhibit symptoms of mental health issues or even be prone to substance abuse. This is where the codependent wants to come in and rescue them but is faced with continuous rejection. This hot and cold dynamic makes for an extremely intense—but simultaneously extremely toxic—chemistry between the two that neither of them would want to let go of.

The Cycle of Narcissism and Codependency

We often tend to think of narcissists and codependents as polar opposites because of the basic narcissistic trait of apparent excessive selfishness and self-love that contrasts with the core codependency trait of excessive selflessness and self-sacrifice. However, according to a study, narcissism and codependency have a lot more in common than is apparent (Irwin, 1995).

Both narcissists and codependents need to feel needed. Their sense of fulfillment comes from others, not from within themselves. Both have been disconnected from their true selves. Both operate from a place of internalized shame, even though they may cope with it differently. While codependents cope with their shame by trying to become excessively useful to others and seeking their love, narcissists cope with it by inflating their apparent worth, trying to dominate others, and seeking control over them. Narcissists, like codependents, have an unhealthy sense of boundaries. Both of them operate by mirroring issues without trying to think objectively about them—by using blame. While narcissists blame others for their issues, codependents always tend to blame themselves for others' problems. Both of them have problems identifying and asserting their feelings and opinions effectively. Like codependents, narcissists rely on criticism, labels, and demands. When they express their opinions, they are usually rigid about their beliefs and lack respect for any differences of opinions. Both seek control over others' lives. Codependents seek to control their partners by relinquishing their personal boundaries and allowing their resources to be taken advantage of, thereby acting as the rescuer who knows what's best. Narcissists, on the other hand, will seek control through manipulation, lies, and people-pleasing, if it comes down to it. Because of their unhealthy behaviors, both narcissists and codependents struggle to form true bonds of intimacy.

Since narcissists use arrogance as their coping mechanism, their true healing can only happen by learning humility. Because codependents use self-hatred as their coping mechanism for their internal shame, their true healing can only occur when they learn to develop a healthy sense of self-esteem and self-love.

When noting the above comparisons, it must be remembered that while all narcissists are codependents, most codependents are *not* narcissists. In fact, most codependents are empathetic—a connection we will explore in the coming sections.

Childhood Trauma and People-Pleasing Tendencies

When we think of a trauma response, the first thing that comes to mind is the fight-or-flight response or even the fight-or-freeze response. However, there is a fourth, rarely talked about, trauma response called "fawning" that many of us are unaware of. This trauma response is a way of diffusing conflict by fundamentally seeking out what the other person wants and giving in to their demands to feel safe and secure in the said relationship. Long story short, it refers to people-pleasing tendencies when you are feeling insecure in a relationship.

Fawning—or people-pleasing—occurs when an individual has internalized shame or anger toward themselves. They tend to overcompensate for this by agreeing and giving in to every demand that people make of them and taking on more than they can handle, even if they are on the verge of burnout. They struggle with personal boundaries and because of this, they often get taken advantage of by others, especially by people whom they care for. They struggle to form opinions of their own, even when asked for them, and tend to form codependent relationships.

Fawning, as a trauma response, can rear its ugly head in many ways. Some of them are discussed below.

- Basing one's thoughts, opinions, and emotions on someone else's.
- Struggling to figure out one's emotions.
- Lost or very vague sense of self.
- Always attempting to please other people, often at the cost of one's own happiness, like canceling one's plans because one is invited

elsewhere, trying to be too agreeable by compromising one's values and following someone else's even if they are contradictory, etc.

- Automatically trying to calm the other person down by any means possible at the first sign of disagreement.
- Having difficulty revealing your authentic self to people and feeling like no one really knows you.
- Experiencing difficulty saying "no."
- Bottling up emotions and venting them least expectedly, or to strangers.
- Feeling guilty immediately after experiencing righteous anger, by immediately reverting to self-blame mode.
- Feeling responsible if someone else is triggered and wanting to take responsibility for everyone else's "potential" triggers, thereby constantly walking on eggshells.
- Feeling disconnected despite being in a crowd or among your social circle.

If you experience these feelings and have people-pleasing tendencies as a trauma response, then know that, although it may seem like a daunting obstacle to overcome—since it is almost like a reflex—you can overcome it by learning to set boundaries, giving up the habit of apologizing and saying "yes" as a reflex. If all else fails, seek professional help to come to terms with your childhood trauma.

The Empath and Codependency

Let us get this straight at the beginning: Empathy is not the same as codependency. An empath is highly sensitive to other people's feelings and energy, and sometimes this sensitivity can feel like a sixth sense. Empaths also absorb other people's energy, which means that they can often end up feeling what the other person is feeling despite not having a romantic, familial, or even platonic bond with them.

On the other hand, a codependent is "someone whose feelings, thoughts, and actions revolve around another person" (Lancer, 2021). This usually happens because the codependent is attached to the person in some way—romantically, platonically, or in a family.

Codependents may center their entire focus on another person without being empathetic to what they are feeling. They might do that just to get an idea of the other person's mood so that they can react accordingly, and not necessarily tune in and put themselves in the other person's shoes. While empaths care about what the other person is feeling, codependents may not necessarily do so, especially if the other person's behavior is hurtful, abusive or if the other person is emotionally closed off, but codependents will still model their behavior depending upon the other person.

Empaths, on the other hand, while being acutely aware of what the other person is feeling, may not be reactive or change their behavior in a way that is centered around the other person. They may care for the person's feelings and may even go so far as to offer help, but if the help costs them their own happiness, they may have a good enough sense of boundaries and self-preservation to withdraw from the person. They may put a distance between themselves and the other person if they sense that they will be abused or unsafe, unlike codependents who remain attached despite the toxicity. So, an empath can exercise their boundaries and not behave like a codependent.

Although empathy and codependency are not interchangeable, most codependents are empaths. Being both a codependent and an empath can be especially challenging for an individual and may leave them at a higher risk of being abused because they can feel their abuser's pain and hurt. If they are unaware that they are highly empathetic, they may confuse this emotional connection with their abuser to be love. Since they are not in touch with their sense of self, it can be harder for them to implement the boundaries they need with a toxic partner. Because they feel the need for love and bonding, they may confuse the initial pursuit and attention given to them by narcissists and personality-disordered people to be love. Their tendency to self-introspect first, whenever there is a conflict and focus on the needs of others, and their forgiving nature, may enable their partner's abusive behavior. Because of their porous boundaries, they may internalize negative energy and toxicity without realizing that it is not their fault.

A good way for empaths to reconnect with their true selves and hold their own space is to learn to recognize what they feel and need; then express and fulfill it. They can also learn to set clear boundaries and work on their self-esteem and self-care skills to recover from their codependent patterns. We will discuss some of these recovery skills in the next part of the book.

PART 2:

OVERCOME! EMOTIONAL REGULATION STRATEGY

CHAPTER 3: YOU COME FIRST

One of the foremost tenets of codependency recovery is learning to prioritize oneself. This is usually the first and most difficult obstacle for a codependent to pass through because it goes against the very core of their codependent behavior—putting their partner's needs before their own, every time and all the time.

In this section, we will explore how to break the patterns of codependency and journey towards forming healthier bonds. True healing cannot happen without an acceptance of all the factors causing the problem. So let us explore some of the roles that *both* codependents and their partners play in pursuing, establishing, and continuing an unhealthy relationship.

Have You Heard of Narcissists? (They Eat Codependents for Breakfast!)

Since both narcissists and codependents have so many overlapping qualities, you may be wondering if you are one too. Fret not. The mere fact that you are willing to reflect and self-introspect is a sign that you probably aren't one. Narcissists lack the empathy that is required to take criticism positively and use it to reflect on their behavior and work on themselves—according to them, they are perfect as they are and they do not need to change. However, even if you are not one, it is very important to identify the traits of a narcissist and the traits that attract you—a codependent—to a narcissist so that you can recognize the dysfunctional behavior patterns that you have been subconsciously following and break the cycle. Doing this will enable you to pursue healthier relationships with emotionally secure individuals.

For an individual to be diagnosed as a narcissist (the real deal with Narcissistic Personality Disorder, not the overused term that gets casually thrown around these days by everyone dealing with any and every toxic person), a mental health professional needs to check at least five of the following criteria in the Diagnostic and Statistical Manual of Mental Disorders, Fifth Edition (Brazier & Sissons, 2020):

1. Do they have a heightened sense of self-importance that can manifest as grandiose delusions?
2. Do they have an obsession with imagined success, power, intelligence, beauty, or ideal love?
3. Do they possess a feeling of being superior or special and a belief that, consequently, they should only associate with other special or high-status individuals or institutions?
4. Do they need admiration constantly and in excess?
5. Do they have an increased sense of self-importance and are prone to entitled behavior?
6. Do they not hesitate to take advantage of others to fulfill their agendas?

7. Do they have no empathy and feel no need to understand others' needs or place themselves in others' shoes?
8. Are they constantly either jealous of others or under the impression that others are jealous of them?
9. Do they tend to display arrogance along with haughty behaviors and temperaments?

Along with the aforementioned "symptoms," narcissists can display the following behaviors that may be noticeable if one knows where and when to look:

- Although narcissists crave admiration and attention excessively, they do so because they have a very weak or non-existent sense of self-esteem so they end up feeling extremely disappointed when they do not receive the admiration that they crave.
- Although they have fragile self-esteem, they will come across as extremely self-confident because of their outward display of superiority.
- Due to their superiority complex, they may exaggerate their acquaintanceship with wealthy or prominent individuals.
- This sense of superiority may also lead them to overestimate their achievements and skills while undervaluing the achievements of others.
- They may come across as very charming at the outset but may become annoyed or angry very quickly if things do not go their way.

- You will find them taking a lot of trouble to voice their issues but they will show little to no regard for the issues of others.
- Whenever their fragile ego is threatened, they will behave aggressively, also termed "Narcissist Rage."
- They have an extremely hard time dealing with failure and disappointment, usually ending up with an extreme sense of shame, humiliation, and emptiness.
- When they fear that they may not succeed at something, they will be extremely hesitant to give it a try because they do not want to risk failure and the associated sense of shame, even in the slightest amount.
- They cannot sustain healthy relationships and even the unhealthy ones will eventually fail because they are so self-centered.
- They are usually alienated and emotionally disconnected from most people, and will only usually surround themselves with people who offer them their much-needed admiration.
- They have very inconsistent performances in their academic and professional lives—they are either high achievers because of their overconfidence or perform poorly when they are faced with failure or criticism due to a lack of healthy self-esteem, or experience an on-and-off combination of both extremes.
- They may be suspicious of people's motives and have extreme trust issues, usually accompanied by a mindset that everyone is out to get them. This usually stems from a false but heightened sense of self-importance because they think that everything revolves around them.

- They may be socially very withdrawn because of their self-esteem issues. Note that this is not the same as introversion, where they can interact socially but can spend time alone with themselves and recharge. Narcissists withdraw from situations where they feel they may not receive the attention that they crave.
- They have extreme difficulty managing emotions and can behave in a volatile manner. Tense situations involving narcissists can escalate in toxicity extremely quickly because narcissists love to fuel the drama.

It is to be noted that despite all these descriptive guidelines for narcissistic behavior, it is ill-advised to self-diagnose someone as a narcissist (having Narcissist Personality Disorder) unless you are a certified health professional. However, if you suspect someone of being a narcissist, it is best to use boundaries and coping mechanisms to steer clear of them and avoid their toxicity. Since codependents have a weak sense of boundaries, narcissists innately sense that this would be the perfect prey for them.

Why Narcissists Are Drawn to Codependents

One might wonder why narcissists almost always seem to prey only on codependents. This notion is, however, incorrect. Narcissists approach everybody with their self-centered tactics and toxic traits. However, they fail to attract—and also find unattractive—people who are emotionally healthy, secure, and authentic. The narcissist-codependent dynamic works—although it is not sustainable and eventually becomes very toxic and abusive—because codependents have an equal role to play in it.

As mentioned earlier, narcissists come into contact with different kinds of people. However, they cannot tolerate emotionally secure, authentic people who practice healthy boundaries because that would mean a loss of the control they want to establish in the relationship. Similarly, emotionally healthy people might be equally turned off by the narcissist's constant disrespect of boundaries and their tendency to display volatile and exaggerated behavior. However, when a narcissist meets a codependent, the codependent's subconscious willingness to let them overstep boundaries and take control of the relationship feels just right for the narcissist. The codependent, on the other hand, is initially attracted by the seemingly confident facade of someone who apparently has got their act together along with the initial generous displays of affection.

When they enter into a relationship, everything works out beautifully, initially, because the codependent loves to sacrifice their own needs for those of their partner and is proud of their ability to put their partner before themselves, while the narcissist loves receiving unconditional care without having to give anything in return. However, as the relationship progresses, the codependent realizes that they have been giving everything to the relationship without receiving anything in return. They start harboring feelings of resentment because, deep down, they still feel the need to be loved and appreciated—something which the narcissist will never give them. The narcissist, on the other hand, continues to take advantage of their partner and use them to meet their own needs without giving up anything in return because this is just how they want it to be. They refuse to change, leaving the codependent bitter and angry. Despite their inner resentment, codependents have a tendency to self-blame, convinced that no one can love them for who they are rather than what they have to offer to others, so they continue to remain in the toxic relationship with the narcissist.

How Codependency Steals Your Identity

The main reason why codependency is such an unhealthy state to be in is that it has several characteristics that cause the individual to lose their sense of self and identity. Some of them are listed below.

Issues with Recognizing and Communicating One's Needs, Opinions, and Emotions

Most codependents were taught to neglect their own needs during their formative years. Because of this, they struggle to recognize what they are feeling, thinking, or wanting. They may have no strong opinion of their own on certain issues and when they do, they may feel intimidated to voice them because they have been taught to believe that doing so is selfish. Due to this, they may often twist the facts to fit others' perspectives and hesitate to state what they *really* feel.

Feeling Responsible for Others' Well-Being and Emotions

Another major trait codependents possess, that weakens their sense of self, is that they feel an excessive sense of responsibility for other people's well-being and emotions. They may feel that it is their duty to "save" their partner from themselves and may even feel worthless in a healthy relationship where their partner does not require any sort of rescuing. This sense of responsibility may also make them feel personally responsible for their partner's negative state of mind, even if it has nothing to do with them in actuality. They often suffer from severe anxiety because of this since they often find themselves walking on eggshells so as not to accidentally hurt anyone in any way possible.

Difficulty Saying "No"

Codependents are so used to putting others' needs over their own that they often accept requests to help people at the expense of their own well-being. They want to please others at any cost because their entire sense of purpose and happiness depends on it. They will often refrain from doing certain things they love altogether if they feel that they may be disappointing someone by doing so.

Weak Sense of Boundaries

One of the chief qualifying traits that someone lacks a sense of self is a lack of boundaries. Boundaries often become porous when the line between what we are responsible for and what others are responsible for, gets blurry. This means that codependents will often let others take advantage of their resources and maybe even their bodies because they cannot place limitations on what part of themselves others should have access to and shouldn't, since this was never taught to them as children. Even when they know deep down that they are being violated, they have been programmed to suffer in silence rather than take a stand for themselves.

Self-Esteem Issues

Codependents' self-esteem issues usually manifest as a belief that they do not deserve to be in a healthy relationship or treated any better than they are, in their current toxic relationships. Since they do not have a defined sense of self or healthy self-esteem to define their identity, they may often seek out solace in predefined social roles of being a parent, partner, spouse, manager, employee, etc.

Tendency to Obsess Over and Control Relationships

Codependents tend to have an unhealthy level of obsession with the relationships that they are in because of their extreme dependency on their partner for their sense of self and identity. They have extreme anxiety issues because they fear abandonment and being left alone by their partner. This is one of the reasons that they may be unable to leave toxic and abusive relationships, despite being unhappy.

Living in Denial and Despair

Codependents are simultaneously desperate for the world to love them for what they are while hiding their authentic selves from everyone. This can cause them intense grief and anxiety. They may also indulge in a lot of direct or indirect dishonesty. They may do this by lying about their true feelings, opinions, or needs. They may also indulge in indirect dishonesty by withholding information that can cause discomfort or displeasure to their partners. This inauthenticity may also cause them to be perpetually anxious or depressed.

You Can't Pour from an Empty Cup

In a society where remaining stoic in the face of pain and hurt is considered a virtue, it can be a curse for codependents who silently drain themselves—as their toxic partners leech everything off them—without ever complaining until they have nothing left to give; not even to themselves, to relieve them of their pain and silent suffering. Codependents keep emptying their cup for everyone else. They barely get to refill it before someone else comes along with yet another request that they cannot refuse. This ultimately drains them dry.

As a society, we celebrate those who hustle and keep rolling with the punches, never stopping to ask if they are doing okay. Too often, even emotionally healthy people find themselves putting off self-care when they get too busy. Making it through the day takes priority over pausing for a few minutes to check in with oneself. Although bringing your attention to self-care, especially during your most busy phases in life, may seem paradoxical (*I already have so much to deal with. Do five minutes of self-care even make a difference? Shouldn't I just put it off until I feel up to it?*)

it actually helps you use the rest of your time more productively. However, it is best to check in if you need self-care sooner rather than later so that you can always keep your cup full and keep giving without emptying your cup and falling into resentment and despair. The following table should help you understand how full or empty your cup is.

Percentage of your cup being full	**How you feel during this phase**
-50 to -100%	Complete havoc ➢ Do you feel as if your life is a complete mess? ➢ Do you feel as if things are simply spiraling out of control? ➢ Do you feel as if life just keeps throwing you curveballs and you spend all your time deflecting them? ➢ Do you feel as if you are constantly in damage control mode and constantly in a state of anxiety because of it? ➢ Do you feel as if you have no time or resources to dedicate to taking care of yourself or prioritizing your own needs? ➢ Do you find yourself resorting to addictions (that could be anything from substance abuse to something seemingly harmless as gaming) or coping mechanisms that help you escape reality? ➢ Do you find it impossible to show generosity to others since you don't even seem to have time for yourself? If any of this sounds familiar to you, then it is high time that you asked for help. Seek professional help or a social support system to help you with your current situation because you are clearly overwhelmed. Start using the time you gain to plan to change the path that you are on, even if it is just five minutes a day, and even if the change in direction is gradual. With consistency, you will be able to create a shift in your life.

-25 to -50%	At the edge of the cliff ➢ Do you feel perennial fatigue or illness of some sort? ➢ Do you find yourself constantly putting off your self-care needs until the "ideal day" comes along, whether it may be the weekend or the annual vacation? ➢ Are you on some sort of medication to get yourself through the day (even if it is just popping some pills for your chronic headaches)? ➢ Does handing out favors cause you to be angry and resentful, and drain you? If you just said, *Welcome to my life,* then you are probably stuck in a vicious cycle of mental drain. Despite the medication, I'll stick my neck out here and go ahead and tell you that it is probably more of a psychological barrier that you are facing. Since you do not have the energy to improve your current situation, you are probably talking yourself out of whatever it is that you need to do, to turn things around for yourself—because maintaining the status quo seems infinitely easier. In such cases, seek out your support system and make time for self-care. This catalyst will eventually turn into a positive domino effect that will help you recharge.
0 to -25%	Breaking point ➢ Does your life feel dull and dreary, as if you are on a boring, repeating loop every day? ➢ Do you feel like you have just enough mental energy to get you through the day, yet you yearn for a challenge or excitement? ➢ Do you feel like you could do with a peaceful break from your routine? ➢ Do you feel like entertaining others' requests depletes you of whatever little energy you have left so that at the

	end of the day, you feel like you have nothing left for yourself? If you feel like this is your life right now, it is time to self-reflect and introspect about what you are feeling and what you really want in life. It is time to rediscover yourself and your short-term and long-term goals, and then work to align your reality with said goals.
0 to 50%	Just *so* tired ➢ Do you find yourself noticing certain repeating patterns in your life that leave you feeling trapped? ➢ Have you had self-awareness of what works for you and what does not, and you find yourself willing to move on from whatever is holding you back from achieving your full potential? ➢ Do you find that you can be creative at times but cannot yet maintain consistency? ➢ Do you find yourself willing to make time to give to others but you need some time after, to rest and recoup? If you find yourself answering "Yes" to the aforementioned questions, then you are probably already on the path to recovery. Seeking professional advice could help you make that leap forward and steer yourself in the right direction.
50 to 100%	Going ➢ Do you feel like you are mostly healthy and in alignment with your inner goals, despite minor hiccups along the way? ➢ Do you feel a positive energy and a positive mindset coursing through you most of the time? ➢ Do you find yourself being able to consistently create something new?

	➢ Do you feel like you have achieved the perfect balance between giving to others and attending to your own needs? If your answer to the above was a resounding "Yes," then pat yourself on the back for managing to keep your cup filled!
100%	On top of your game ➢ Do you feel nourished and rested—physically, mentally, and spiritually? ➢ Do you find that you are making great progress toward your goals and have made peace with the things that are not under your control? ➢ Do you feel completely comfortable in your own skin? ➢ Do you feel that you are not just using your talents for your own benefit, but also for those who are around you, and that gives you a sense of fulfillment? ➢ Do you feel your creativity flowing and there is a lot more where it came from? ➢ Do you feel generous towards those around you without feeling depleted? If you find yourself in this state then know that you are at the top of your game and make the most of it, conquer new frontiers, and achieve greatness, while you're at it!

The Pushover Syndrome

The pushover syndrome is a common trait that can be found in most codependent individuals. One might wonder how someone can allow another person to walk all over them and push them around. We might even feel indignant when we observe such behavior occurring in front of us, vowing that if it were us, we would never allow ourselves to be trampled over like that.

In reality, we have all been a pushover at some point or the other, even if it is for a brief period. While it is important to pick one's battles and let the more trivial things in life slide when aiming to achieve the bigger ones, it is also important to make sure that our tendency to be a pushover does not turn into a habit.

There are many reasons why one could be a perpetual pushover. Your childhood may have been full of toxic adults who shut you down anytime you tried to assert yourself so that in time, allowing everyone to push you around became the norm.

Another reason could be that you are codependent, and being a pushover is just part of the package that has been passed down along with the other generational curses for you to unpack. Self-esteem issues also play an important part in turning people into pushovers.

The more you believe you are not worthy of being treated right, the more people will walk over you, resulting in deeper feelings of hopelessness and furthering your tendency to be a pushover—a vicious cycle of low self-esteem and being pushed around, each one perpetuating the other.

There may be instances where—at certain phases in your life—you may feel helpless and thus allow people to push you around and take advantage of you.

Since this is such a slow and insidious response mechanism, we often fail to identify when we have started giving in to people and letting them treat us like doormats. It is important to be self-aware of our behaviors so that we can nip this one in the bud when we see it starting to take hold of us. The following self-assessment can help you become more mindful of your behavior and course-correct before you normalize the pushover syndrome in your life:

1. Do you find that you lack the confidence to speak up for yourself and instead, passively allow people to talk over you?
2. Do you find that you are too timid and fearful to pursue your dreams, goals, or ambitions in life and have difficulty feeling motivated?
3. Do you find that you often soften your stance or change your opinion to accommodate others' positions or views, despite your inner voice screaming at you that you need to speak up?
4. Do you feel that you go around pleasing people to the extent that no one knows who you truly are?
5. Do you feel that you are insincere in the compliments that you hand out to people?
6. Do you feel unfulfilled when you are on your own and need others to fill the void?
7. Do you find yourself overcommitting and overextending yourself constantly, due to prioritizing others' needs above yours?
8. Do you find yourself withholding your true feelings and thoughts because of feelings of inadequacy?
9. Are you always uncertain of how your life is going to unfold because you feel that others have more control over it than you do?
10. Do you feel that you apologize even when it is not your fault, simply because you want to make sure you have not accidentally hurt anyone?

The number of questions that you have answered *yes* to can be quite accurately predictive of how far your pushover syndrome has taken hold. If you have answered in the positive to

0-1 questions: Congratulations! You are not a pushover! You know how to establish boundaries and make yourself heard.

2-4 questions: You are not an all-out pushover just yet but you experience the occasional moment of uncertainty. You may be on the verge of being a pushover. Working on your self-esteem at this stage can help you become more self-aware of your own identity and take a stand for it.

5 or more questions: You are being treated like a doormat and you probably know it already. The good news is that you can overcome the pushover syndrome and start taking a stand for yourself.

One of the first things you will have to do to start standing up for yourself is to be honest with yourself about what you want to do and what you do not. That inner voice that tells you to refuse? Listen to it and listen closely. You'll thank yourself for it later. Once you have learned to recognize your thoughts and emotions, the next step is to learn to express them honestly. If you fear that you would be hurting the person in question by expressing your thoughts that are in contrast with theirs, you can choose a safe space for the discussion. Pick a one-on-one private space where you can be sure you won't be embarrassing them by contradicting them openly. However, always remember that you have all the right to express your thoughts—that's half the battle won.

Also, learn to refuse people when you are already feeling on edge. Remember that "no" here is to protect you, rather than to reject them. If you want to soften the blow for them, you can offer them alternatives that they could resort to instead of depending on you, since you are unavailable. In this way, you know that you have done all you can while simultaneously protecting your sacred space. It is important to often be direct and upfront about these things rather than beat around the bush. This allows the other person to gain clarity of what you expect and react accordingly. By being direct, you are being authentic, both to yourself and the other party. This is especially important when you go on to set boundaries.

When dealing with toxic people, remember that you are not the only one they might have tried to take advantage of. Toxic people test everyone, but they stick around those who have weak boundaries because they subconsciously know that they have found the perfect prey. Make sure to set firm boundaries and stick to them.

Finally, understand and accept that each individual is unique and everyone has their own path to take in this journey called life. What one person perceives as the norm may not be so for another. Once you understand this and accept your journey for its uniqueness, you have opened the path to resist the urge to let people trample all over you and overcome the pushover syndrome.

Ever Tried Prioritizing Yourself?

Although many people realize at some point in their lives that they need to prioritize themselves, there can often be many social and psychological barriers preventing them from doing so. Our society celebrates martyrs.

"Oh, wow! He gave up his job to take care of his kids!"

"It's wonderful how they make time for everyone in their family"

"What an amazing partner you are—to be able to give up such a big opportunity for your partner's convenience!"

We've heard them all—either being spoken to us or to someone we know.

Despite these barriers, it is important to remember that self-care is essential. It's a necessity, not a luxury. This is because when we feel completely drained, we will have nothing to offer to others. While we may continue with the daily drudgery that is our routine, we will not feel the happiness that we used to while we were pouring from a full cup. This is because doing what we love fills our cup. This is not selfishness, this is simply self-preservation. We often drain ourselves because of the glorified hustle culture. However, the daily hustle can often cause us to forget our true goals and the little things that give us true joy.

This may also cause us to start relying on others and infiltrating their boundaries. When we cannot meet our own needs, we often drain others' energy too. We let our inner critic take over and ultimately find that we are more guided by negativity than productivity. We become resentful and unrealistic in our expectations of ourselves. When we cannot be compassionate to ourselves, we forget to be compassionate to others, which is why we not only end up hurting ourselves but also those close to us. This is why self-compassion and prioritizing oneself are important. When maintained, we show up as better versions of ourselves and can motivate and uplift those around us.

After you have realized that it is necessary to take care of yourself before taking care of others, the next mental block to overcome will be the negative beliefs that are holding you back. Negative thought patterns that limit your potential or cause you to expect perfectionism from yourself could cause you to be stopping you from showing up as your best self. While the former holds you back from initiating your goals, the latter keeps you stuck in a perpetual loop of rethinking and overthinking, instead of moving on to higher goals. These limiting beliefs are often a result of trying to conform to other people's expectations of us.

To prioritize yourself, one of the first things to let go of is trying to fulfill all the expectations that others have of you. By letting go of these, you can forge your own path in life and find alignment with your inner self. This is the first step of your journey to growing and improving yourself as a person.

CHAPTER 4:
OVERCOMING FEAR OF ABANDONMENT

"Fear of abandonment is the overwhelming worry that people close to you will leave."

(PIETRANGELO, 2019)

It may develop in childhood as a result of loss or neglect or as the result of a traumatic adult relationship. Anyone can develop a fear of abandonment at any point in their lives and it could impact potential relationships in the future if one does not recognize and overcome it. Let us find out what it is and how it works so that we can learn to overcome it and lead happier lives.

How Fear of Abandonment Works

For an individual to grow into an emotionally healthy person, their physical and emotional needs must be met in their formative years. When these needs are not met, it can result in the individual developing a fear of abandonment. The reason for these needs going unmet could be many—the death of a parent, parental abuse, living in extreme poverty, rejection by peers, witnessing a prolonged illness or death of a loved one, abandonment or betrayal by a romantic partner could all be possible causes of abandonment issues faced by an individual. It could also be caused by personality disorders such as avoidant personality disorder, borderline personality disorder, or separation anxiety disorder.

Fear of abandonment can have far-reaching effects on the life of the affected individual that can include self-esteem issues, trust issues, anger management issues, difficulty regulating emotions leading to mood swings, codependent tendencies, intimacy issues, depression, trouble sustaining friendships and romantic relationships, anxiety issues, and panic disorders. Hence, this must be addressed and overcome. But now the question arises: How does one know if one has a fear of abandonment? Here is a self-assessment to help you evaluate if you have abandonment issues so that you can self-evaluate and seek necessary help if you need to.

1. Do you find yourself getting attached to people too quickly, thinking that they may just leave you and find someone better if you do not form a bond with them?
2. Do you find yourself detaching yourself from those whom you care for—just as quickly—at the first signs of trouble in the relationship, to avoid getting hurt?
3. Do you find yourself going out of your way to please people because you do not want to risk displeasing them, resulting in them distancing themselves from you?
4. Do you find it difficult to accept criticism and feel extremely hurt when someone does so, even if it is constructive?
5. Do you feel devastated when someone gets upset with you?

6. Does even the notion that you may accidentally hurt someone scare you?
7. Do you find it difficult to make friends unless you are sure that they like you?
8. Do you find yourself indulging in self-blame when a relationship does not work out?
9. Do you have difficulty controlling your emotions when someone hurts you, and it makes you extremely upset or angry?
10. Do you find yourself getting overly clingy, the more your partner asks for space?
11. Do you often feel jealous, suspicious, or critical of your partner?
12. Do you constantly feel that you are not good enough, not desirable enough, or have other feelings of inadequacy?
13. Do you find yourself constantly worrying about what other people may think of you, what opinion they may form about you, or what flaws they might notice in you?
14. Do you find yourself consistently getting involved in unhealthy or toxic relationships?
15. Do you find that you continue to stay in a relationship, even if it is making you unhappy, simply because you do not believe in letting go of people?
16. Do you find it difficult to commit to a relationship, whether it is in the form of hesitating to define the relationship for what it is at present or what it could potentially be in the future?

If you find yourself answering "yes" to more than half of the above questions, you may be struggling with fear of abandonment. Read on to find out how you can overcome this fear and form healthier, happier relationships.

Fear of Abandonment and Codependency

Although fear of abandonment is not a diagnosable disorder on its own, it can be identified as a major symptom of other underlying issues including codependency. At the crux of codependency lies a fear of abandonment, rooted in an insecure attachment style. Although they cannot be used interchangeably—since codependency is not the only personality disorder that has a foundational issue of fear of abandonment—there are a lot of common traits that both these dysfunctional conditions share. For starters, both codependency and fear of abandonment have common roots in childhood emotional needs going unmet. Both lead to people-pleasing, and an inability to let go of toxic relationships. Both dysfunctions cause the individuals suffering from the issue to experience extreme inadequacy, inferiority, and low self-worth. This can be so extreme that they tend to feel grateful even for the unhealthy attention they get from toxic individuals and tolerate behavior that an emotionally healthy individual would find highly unacceptable. They feel that no one else will love them if they leave the current relationship. Because of this, they continue to stay in their unhealthy relationship. So overcoming this fear can prove to be a major spark of growth for those struggling with codependency.

How to Overcome Your Fear of Abandonment

To overcome your fear of abandonment and reclaim your identity, keep in mind the following:

- Stop blaming yourself for feeling this way. Remember that you did not choose to have this fear of abandonment—it chose you. Now you are having to deal with something that you had no control over, previously. The fact that you are willing to take responsibility and take back control is applaudable. Pat yourself on the back for that and take your first step forward on this journey to freedom.
- Acknowledge that fear is a normal human emotion. We all have fears. This is not a sign of weakness—it is just a sign of being human. So give yourself some self-love and self-compassion and avoid being too hard on yourself.
- Understand that you have no control over when and how you experience insecurity, but you have control over what you do with it. Instead of seeking out your partner—or anyone else—to quell your insecure feelings, take charge of managing them yourself.
- This implies taking full responsibility when the fear of abandonment strikes your heart, instead of expecting your partner to fix it for you, even if they triggered it.
- When you find yourself detaching yourself for fear of being abandoned, promise yourself that you will use this fear to make yourself emotionally resilient and self-reliant.
- Show up to your partner with the newfound confidence that you have achieved with this new sense of responsibility for yourself.

- Remember that recovery from abandonment issues will not just come to you and integrate itself into your life. You have to make conscious efforts towards a systematic recovery by consistently choosing to be emotionally self-reliant.
- Once you have integrated the belief that you are responsible for fixing your fears and insecurities, make conscious changes in your behavior that aligns with that belief. The moment you seek out your partner to resolve your fears for you, and they refuse, you are giving away your power.
- Be compassionate and patient with yourself. Fear of abandonment is a very powerful emotion and not an easy behavioral dysfunction to overcome. It has deep trauma and hurt attached to it so it is important to set realistic expectations for yourself. No one can overcome it overnight. The recovery from fear of abandonment is an ongoing process that will bear fruits over time with consistency.
- Although it is important to forgive yourself for your lapses, it is equally important to pay mindful attention to them, and course-correct immediately if you find yourself falling back into the pattern of relying on your partner for reassurance. Remember that forgiveness does not mean allowing yourself to be slack.
- Remember that there is freedom and self-discovery at the end of the tunnel and that all your hard work and efforts will be paid off with you gaining sovereignty over your individuality and identity.

Will I Be Okay After Leaving a Codependent Relationship?

The short answer: "Yes! You can be and you *will* be!" The long answer: "It may not be the easiest thing to do, but you will get there, eventually, with time, and this section is to help you do just that."

The following tips can help you survive after breaking up from a codependent relationship:

Seek Support

Humans are social beings. We all need support and validation from those whom we care for and whose opinions matter to us. It is important to remember that while trying to unlearn codependency one does not have to be completely isolated to undo codependent patterns. Just because you are trying to overcome an unhealthy attachment does not mean you have to shift to the other extreme of the spectrum and completely shun social interactions. Instead, seek out your friends and family and spend some time with them—while respecting their time boundaries. Seeking out the company of emotionally healthier individuals will help you unlearn toxic behaviors and learn emotionally secure ones in their stead.

Establish Boundaries

Weak or porous boundaries go hand in hand with people-pleasing and fear of abandonment. We allow others to cross certain thresholds because we fear that refusing them will be met with retaliation in the form of rejection or abandonment. While this may hold for some individuals in your life, you need to always remember that it is worthwhile letting such individuals go. This is because what you gain from letting them go is your sense of individuality, alignment with your inner self, and a deep sense of happiness and freedom.

Seek Professional Help

If you find yourself unable to break the unhealthy patterns, or if you feel that you do not have a good support system of healthy individuals in your life, then it may be a good idea to seek out a mental health professional to provide some objective insights into the situation. Be prepared to work on your negativity and make the necessary changes in your life when working with a professional.

Join a Support Group

You can also seek out a support group of individuals who are experiencing similar struggles in life, to help you validate your experiences and prevent you from becoming isolated. It is important to stay connected and fulfill your social needs, especially after a breakup. Human connection is very important while we are in the process of healing ourselves.

Reevaluate Your Needs

One of the best ways to break patterns is to retrospectively identify common behaviors that have been repeated in your past relationships, be it family or romantic. When we deal with abusive family members, it is natural to consciously try and make efforts not to get trapped with similar toxic people again and again. However, if you find that they are repeating regardless, it is important to understand our own role in allowing them the freedom to do so, identifying their roots, and repairing core issues that lie deep within our subconscious. This ensures that our subconscious mind does not puppeteer our conscious behaviors from the shadows, leading us into toxic relationships repeatedly.

Be Compassionate with Yourself

It is very tempting to be hard on oneself and fall into negative thinking patterns when trying to deal with the withdrawal that comes with breaking up from a codependent relationship. However, it is important to show compassion and love to yourself despite acknowledging your role in enabling toxic patterns. Remember that this was not your fault—you were born and raised into this curse that has been passed down through generations in your family to your parents and finally to you. Your step towards breaking it is an achievement as it stands. Remember to go easy on yourself if you experience brief relapses because no one is perfect.

Enjoy Your Own Company

Falling into rebound relationships is easy for those who have codependent tendencies. Remember, no matter how much your inner voice shouts, "This is the right one, finally!" avoid the temptation to enter into another relationship. If it is the "right" person, they will understand that you are in the process of healing and wait for your stars to align before pursuing the relationship further. Entering into a relationship even with an emotionally healthy person before you are healed and mindful of your relationships can start another cycle of toxicity—something which you're trying to avoid now, not continue.

Stay Away from Your Ex

This may be the hardest step, especially if you have children or common friends together. However, know that it can and must be done for the sake of your mental well-being. Going back to your ex will start the old cycle of toxicity all over again. Just remind yourself that if anything had had to improve, it would have been done already and you wouldn't have needed to break up in the first place. The fact that nothing changed during the time you were together should tell you volumes about what is going to happen should you return to the relationship.

Removing Yourself from Codependency and Narcissistic Relationships

The relationship between a codependent and a narcissist is never a healthy one. However, although the codependent is unhappy, they may find it difficult to leave the relationship. Narcissists can come across as very charming and loving at the beginning of the relationship, to codependents, because of their love-bombing techniques. Due to this, combined with the blame-shifting that narcissists lay on their codependent partners, the codependent may spend a significant amount of time, even years, trying to bring the person with whom they fell in love back. Little do they know that such a person never existed—it was only a ploy by the narcissist to secure the supply of unlimited admiration and affection they so desperately crave from the codependent.

Codependents may also become trauma-bonded to their abusive partner during this time. Even after repeated abuse, the codependent may crave those sporadic moments of love that the narcissist partner has shown them. The codependent does not just fear pushback, they may also be more worried about how they would fare without their partner. In fact, because of their affinity and value for undying loyalty, they may feel that the emotional loss is more hurtful than the abuse they will face if they try to break away from the relationship. This may cause them to feel confused and trapped in the relationship.

Even when the codependent does gather the courage to leave the relationship, the narcissist partner will continue with their mind games and drama. They may do this in the form of showering their now estranged partner with the love and affection from before to pretend that they have turned over a new leaf and are sorry for what happened. Alternatively, or perhaps even simultaneously, they may go on to slander their estranged partner in front of their family and friends—basically, anyone who will listen and side with them against their victim. They may even resort to stalking and hoovering to try and suck the codependent back into the relationship. Alternatively, they may try manipulation techniques like trying to make their partner jealous by posting and sharing pictures of themselves with someone new.

Whatever they do, it is important to remember, at this stage, that they are not doing this because they have a healthy love for their partner. They are doing this because their fragile ego is extremely hurt and they are humiliated because of their partner leaving them. Their mind tells them, *After all, how can anyone even consider leaving and moving on from such a perfect partner?*

Once a codependent realizes that their narcissistic partner can never truly love them and their love will never be reciprocated, only then can they truly break up and move on and gain true freedom from the relationship. When this happens, the narcissist may either go ballistic and become vindictive because they have "lost" despite their best manipulative efforts, or they may find a new source to supply them with the admiration they need. If this happens, it is important to remember that once you have moved on, you have moved on and it is not your business to bother about what they are doing. Whether they are happy or sad is immaterial. You are free from a toxic relationship and that is all that matters.

The following pointers can help you reclaim your autonomy and self-esteem once you have decided to break up and move on from a narcissist-codependent relationship:

- Enlist yourself in a support group that preferably involves a therapist.

- Seek out the help of friends who can be empathetic and validating of your traumatic experience instead of simply indulging in ex-bashing or acting judgy towards you for sticking around with your ex for as long as you did.
- Reclaim your autonomy by exploring and reconnecting with your hobbies, friends, work, and other interests. Regardless of your relationship status in the future, you will need a fulfilling life of your own to be happy.
- Work on your self-esteem. Reevaluate your expectations, thoughts, and emotions and learn to honor them.
- Learn to trust your reality and overcome the self-doubt and guilt that you have, both as a result of your codependence as well as your ex's gaslighting behavior.
- Learn to assert your reality and establish boundaries.
- Learn self-care and self-love.
- Traumatic relationships cause us to develop triggers. Recognize the ways that you have been abused and your triggers. Learn to let go of this baggage. You cannot have an emotionally healthy and secure relationship while you still carry the baggage from your past toxic relationships.
- If you fear physical harm and abuse, seek help from the authorities immediately. Remember: Once a physical abuser, always a physical abuser. Don't wait for the violence or peril to escalate. Research the cycle of violence and take appropriate measures to protect yourself.
- Follow through on your word. Remember that if you do not honor your word, no one else will either. When you say you are

leaving, make sure you have thought it out and follow through with it—leave the relationship and do not look back, because if you do, your words lose their value and your partner will take you for granted.

- If you are in a marriage and have to deal with a divorce, make sure you hire good legal counsel. Know that meditation and reconciliation are not good options in the face of previous instances of abuse, so make sure to stand your ground on this matter.
- Irrespective of who initiated the breakup or which partner cemented it, allow yourself to grieve and heal from the loss you are experiencing. Give yourself time to rest and recoup.
- Go no-contact, no exceptions. The only possible exception should be if it is required for co-parenting, in which case, make sure to keep it strictly text-based and use only court-approved apps for communication that can maintain all records of communication.

Now that you know how to break free from a toxic relationship, the next step is to use this newfound freedom to remodel yourself into the wonderful person you have the potential to be. By doing this you can then find the love and relationship that you truly deserve and who can love you back with the same effort that you love them.

FREE GOODWILL

People who help others experience a higher level of fulfillment in life, live longer and make more money. I would like to offer this value to you during this reading or listening experience.

In order to do so, I have a simple question for you. Would you help someone you never met, if it didn't cost you money but you never got credit for it? If so, I haven't asked on behalf on someone you do not know and likely never will.

But they are just like you, or like you were a few years ago. Less experienced, full of desire to help the world, seeking information but unsure where to look. This is where you come in.

The only way me and my team can accomplish our mission to help as many people as possible is by first reaching them. As a small publisher, most people do judge a book on its cover and reviews.

If you have found this book valuable so far, would you please take a brief moment and leave an honest review of the book and its contents?

In order for us to help as many people as possible, reviews are the driving force of how we can better reach people. It will cost you $0 and will take less than 60 seconds.

Your review will have helped one more person who is struggling. One more client who will experience a transformation who otherwise we would have not encountered. One more life changed for the better.

To make that happen all you have to do, and this takes less than 60 seconds, is leave a review.

If you feel good about helping others who are struggling, then you are my kind of person. I am now excited to help you crush it in the upcoming chapters.

PS: If you introduce something valuable to someone, they will associate that value to you. If you like goodwill directly from someone you know who is struggling, then send this book their way. Thank you from the bottom of my heart.

You biggest fan,

Dylan

CHAPTER 5: BUILDING YOUR SELF-WORTH AND SELF-CONFIDENCE

One of the biggest roadblocks to codependents that stands in the way of reclaiming their independence is self-judgment. As the name suggests, self-judgment is the negative self-talk we give ourselves by judging or criticizing ourselves. For a person struggling with codependency, self-judgment can often come as easy as second nature. It could even be a coping mechanism that they use to avoid being hurt by the harsh criticisms of others—by being their own harshest critic before anyone else does.

Examples of negative self-talk are telling yourself you are less intelligent than others, thinking that others take you for a fool for having said or done something, thinking that you can never do anything right, wondering if anyone could ever love you, feeling isolated, and feeling out of place or that you don't belong.

The two main reasons we experience self-judgment are fear of inadequacy and comparison. While the fear of inadequacy is what lies at the heart of self-judgment, the comparison is what drives it. Self-judgment can be summed up as we telling ourselves, "I am not ____ enough, compared to ____," in which the first part, "I am not ____ enough," is the fear talking, while the second half, "compared to ____ " is the comparison talking.

Although all of us have an inner critic—which is normal, by the way—having an overly negative inner voice can cause damage to our mental health and cause us to develop codependent patterns. Beyond a certain healthy threshold, it turns into self-inflicted abuse. Many of us who would never spell out such harsh criticisms to anyone we know do not think twice before saying the same things to ourselves. We need to realize that the words that can destroy others' mental health when spoken out can destroy ours too. Although it is impossible to prevent our inner critic from speaking out, we must learn to deal with it and overcome negative self-talk with enough positive reaffirmations.

Enough with the Self-Judgment

Now that we know where self-judgment stems from and what it looks like, let's find out how to overcome it and improve our self-image and sense of self-worth.

Don't Take It Personally

That's right! As bizarre as it sounds, learn not to take your self-judgment personally. "But I'm the one who is saying these things to myself!" you may protest. Yes and no. Although you are saying these things to yourself, they may not be originating from you. As a codependent empath, you may have been influenced by the negative energy of other people. It is also possible that a particular self-judgmental talk you may be engaging in is caused by a childhood wound on your psyche. Understand that not everything that happens in your mind is from you. There are many external influences at play here and it's up to you to choose what you want to keep and what you need to discard.

Replace It with Self-Love

It is said that one cannot serve two masters at once. Instead of feeding your negative self-judgment, nourish yourself with self-love and positive self-talk. Focus on loving, caring, and accepting yourself for who you are and soon, you will notice that the negative voice is a lot weaker than it used to be and doesn't have the same hold over you anymore. The more you empower the positive voice in your head, the weaker the negative voice becomes.

Too often, the judgment we have for ourselves is also the mentality we have toward others. Showing compassion towards others and practicing giving them the benefit of the doubt may help a great deal to reduce the self-judgment from your inner critic.

Focus on Your Ideal Self

Set goals about the kind of person you would like to become so that you can work towards them instead of pulling yourself down. Ask yourself introspective questions like how your life would be different if you did not have to deal with criticism and self-judgment—how you would look, feel, think, walk, talk, behave, dress, and conduct yourself; what kind of people you would have in your life; where you would live and with whom; how your relationships would play out, etc.

Once you have set these goals for yourself, it will be easier to focus on the direction of these goals rather than falling into the trap of judging yourself for temporary setbacks.

Be Patient

Remember that you will not be able to overcome your self-judgment in a day, two days, or maybe even a week. It may be a continuous work in progress. What you need to look forward to instead is how today is so much better than yesterday and how you can make tomorrow better still. It is alright if things do not go as planned. Taking small steps towards an overarching goal is better than making big leaps and experiencing mental fatigue. Old habits are hard for anyone to break so be patient with yourself and count your blessings for the things that you have accomplished.

Have Faith in Yourself

Have faith in your journey and the decisions that you have made for yourself. Have faith in your accomplishment and your ability to reach your goal. Trust that you are heading in the right direction and trust yourself that you are making progress. It can also help to keep track by keeping a journal and recording your feelings and progress.

Resist the Urge to Compare

Humans love quantifying things. We love to measure and we need a yardstick to measure everything around us. We need that promotion to tell us we have done our job well, and we need grades to tell us how our academic performance has been. Even on social media, we have started measuring our success by the number of people who like what we share.

While it is natural to make comparisons, it is important to make fair comparisons. For example, comparing how your home looks every day to how someone else's picture on social media of how a part of their home looked, even perhaps for a moment, is not a fair comparison. A picture is only the tip of the iceberg and you never know what their homes look like every single day 24/7 to make a comparison. By acknowledging that you are making an unfair comparison, you can stop holding yourself up to unrealistic standards and consequently judging yourself for failing to meet them.

Think Objectively

Learning to overcome irrational beliefs and thinking objectively can go a long way in overcoming self-judgment. We often judge others based on very biased or partial information. Unsurprisingly, we do the same to ourselves. Instead of being quick to jump to conclusions based on the limited information you have about any circumstance, make it a habit to seek out all the facts. Try to hear both sides of the story before passing judgment. If you judge yourself fairly, you can even use your self-judgment to your advantage.

Forgive Yourself

Don't beat yourself up for your self-judgment. If judging yourself was bad enough, you do not need another layer of negativity in your mind to deal with. Remember that self-judgment is inevitable and that everyone has an inner critic that speaks out when it is feeling sassy. The only thing anyone can do about it is to stop it in its tracks and negate the harsh inner critic with self-love and positivity. Don't cause yourself double the hurt by judging yourself for allowing yourself to pass self-judgment!

Consider the Silver Lining

It is said that every cloud has a silver lining. So does self-judgment. As mentioned in the earlier section (Think Objectively), you can use self-judgment to your advantage. It may not always arise out of self-hatred or a low sense of self-worth. It may arise due to one's need for personal growth. In such cases, the inner critic may be acting as a voice of reason and showing you the path to achieve greatness.

Sit With Your Feelings

The most important thing to do when we are in our self-judgment cycle is to notice that we are judging ourselves. Without coming to this realization, we may spiral further down the self-judgment cycle. Once we notice that we are judging ourselves, we can stop to acknowledge our feelings and respond accordingly. Creating the space to be mindful of what you are feeling is very important. Once you do, learn to accept it for what it is. Only then, can you seek out the cause of your self-judgment and respond with self-compassion and self-love to overcome it.

Heal Your Inner Child

One way to overcome your inner critic is to understand where it stems from. Try to ask yourself where the fears came from in the first place. Look back to a younger, more impressionable version of you and ask yourself when the first seed of self-doubt and self-judgment was planted in your mind. Speak to your younger self and reassure them that you have come a long way. Ask yourself this, “If there was one thing I could tell my younger self, what would it be?” Now go ahead and say it to yourself. By showing compassion and healing your inner child, you can also heal your present.

Codependency and Low Sense of Self-Worth

Self-worth can be described as an individual’s true opinion of themselves and how they think of themselves in the absence of external influences. It can also be a measure of how much a person values themselves. When a person has a healthy sense of self-worth, they know their strengths and weaknesses, can set healthy boundaries because they know their limitations, and do not base their opinion of themselves on what other people think of them.

When a person has a low sense of self-worth, they seem to constantly need validation or approval from others to feel valued. Without this influx of validation and affirmations, they start to feel worthless and inadequate. They may also be extremely sensitive to others' opinions of them in the sense that their own opinions of themselves may change based on what others tell them and who they are with.

People with a low sense of self-worth are characterized by people-pleasing tendencies and an extreme dependence on others to fulfill their sense of self-worth. They only feel respected when they can make sacrifices for someone or are needed by the other party in some way. When they find someone that needs them, they start to depend on that person completely and start to build their entire life around the person who needs them. Ironically, it usually turns out that the codependent needs the other person more than they are needed by their partner.

Self-worth and codependency are intricately linked to one another because an individual who has a healthy sense of self-worth is unlikely to depend on others to fill their emotional void.

How Low Self-Confidence Breeds Codependency

A person who has low self-confidence will inevitably start to base their self-worth on external objects and possessions such as money, appearance, social status, academic or professional excellence, etc. Since they do not see value in themselves, they start to look for things outside of themselves that can add that value to their life. Such individuals are usually the ones who end up in codependent relationships because they are more likely to seek their value through their partner's opinion of themselves than their own.

Since they cannot accept themselves, they desperately need their partners to accept them. They start to build their entire lives around their partners. They enmesh themselves and start to see themselves as an extension of their partners. They have trouble seeing themselves as anything outside of their relationship and their entire identity revolves around how valued they are in the relationship. Even though there may be instances when their boundaries are being violated, they will hesitate to speak up because, for them, keeping their partner happy and satisfied takes priority, even at the cost of their happiness. They believe in a black-and-white situation that one must sacrifice for the other to be happy and fail to realize that with proper boundaries, communication, and mutual understanding, there can be a win-win where both partners are happy, as well.

A healthy relationship requires a healthy attachment, intimacy, communication, and boundaries, and a healthy version of all of these requires healthy self-esteem.

How Attachment Style Is Affected by Self-Esteem

An individual's attachment style affects almost everything else about their relationship—the efforts they put into the relationship and pursue their partner, the way they communicate, the level of intimacy they can provide their partner with, and the boundaries they establish and respect. A securely attached individual will be able to show up as their authentic self to their partner and will be very clear about what they require from the relationship. They are aware of what they want in the relationship. When they find someone who meets their needs, they will simply let them know. They will neither play mind games to pursue the person if they are rejected nor will they try to push someone away if the person in question meets their requirements—something which insecurely attached individuals are likely to resort to.

How Boundaries Are Affected by Self-Esteem

Children who come from dysfunctional families have a dysfunctional sense of boundaries that they have developed by observing the dysfunctional behavior of the adults in their family. As children, they may have had their boundaries violated. They may have been controlled, disrespected, had their privacy invaded, been taken advantage of, or scapegoated, due to which their self-esteem takes a massive hit. When they grow up to become adults, they continue to have low self-esteem and a low sense of self-worth. They have difficulty drawing or respecting boundaries. They allow themselves to continue to be treated as poorly as they were treated as kids. Because of this, they continue to perpetuate their toxic cycle in their romantic relationships as adults.

How Communication Is Affected by Self-Esteem

Dysfunctional families lack good communication skills among members—skills that any adult requires if they want to sustain emotionally healthy relationships. Good communication skills are not just a cornerstone of intimate relationships, they are also an indicator of one's self-esteem. This is because healthy relationships require clear, honest, and assertive communication. They also require individuals to be empathetic and active listeners, which is an integral part of good communication. People who have a low sense of self-esteem struggle with communication. This is because they have no idea how to be assertive, as their voices were always dismissed or suppressed as children. Because of this, they hide their true feelings and needs. Instead of communicating openly and honestly with their partner, they resort to assumptions, rhetoric or sarcasm, blaming, lying, criticizing, ignoring, or controlling. This toxic way of communication is a learned behavior from their dysfunctional families and can lead to problems piling up and escalating, instead of being solved.

How Intimacy Is Affected by Self-Esteem

Each individual needs to be autonomous and independent, and simultaneously intimate and attached. Individuality and a sense of self require self-esteem. Each one of us has a unique journey through life and although we enter into relationships, there will be moments when we have to undertake certain pursuits alone. Only when we can pursue our unique journey with confidence can we pursue it with a partner with equal trust. We can only truly love someone else if we are capable of loving ourselves. When we don't love ourselves, the attachment that we have for our partner is not a healthy form of love but rather an unhealthy codependent attachment. True intimacy requires us to be vulnerable in relationships. Only when we are confident about ourselves can we be vulnerable with our partners. When we put up walls and refuse to be vulnerable in relationships, we cannot show up as our authentic selves. We pretend to be someone else, and the whole relationship is nothing but a sham.

Can I Build My Self-Confidence Back Up?

Let us answer the fundamental question first: What is self-confidence and what does a confident person look like? A confident person is someone who stands up for what they believe in, even if it goes against the grain. They are willing to take chances for the things they trust in, acknowledge their mistakes, and grow from them, know how to take a compliment gracefully, and are normally optimistic. From this, we can safely say, "Self-confidence is a feeling of trust in your abilities, qualities, and judgment." (Morin, 2019)

If you find yourself doubting your abilities and judgment, fret not! The good news is that there are many ways that you can build your self-confidence back up. Some of them are listed below.

Acknowledge Your Achievements

Our confidence is directly dependent upon the things that we have achieved. It is easy for our confidence to be lowered when we feel that we haven't yet achieved anything in life, when in reality we may have had significant accomplishments. For very self-critical people, it is easy to forget their accomplishments. One way to keep your confidence levels up is to retrospect at the end of each day and think of three things that you have achieved by adding some value to your life or anyone else's. It may also help to keep a journal to keep track of all the things that you have achieved and look back on it when you are feeling blue so that your confidence levels are always in a healthy state.

Recognize Your Strengths and Weaknesses

Everyone has skills and talents. If you are unsure, ask yourself, "What am I good at? What do I love doing? What do I do best?" Record your answers and try to improve on the skill sets and areas of interest that you excel at. Building on your strengths will give you a confidence boost. Simultaneously, you can also list the things you feel you are not that proficient at—the things that you feel you have less confidence in. You can list them under a separate heading titled, "Things I need to get better at" and use this as input for areas of self-improvement.

Set Goals for Yourself—Both Long-Term and Short-Term

To achieve something, you need to have goals first. Set some goals for yourself, whether they be long-term or short-term goals, whether they be big or small, like simply taking time off for yourself and self-care. Aiming for small, realistic achievements can help boost your confidence.

If you aren't too sure about your goals in life, the following activity might help you become more mindful of the things you want to do and help you achieve them. Make three columns.

In the first column, write down all the things that you would wish to accomplish in your lifetime, no matter how unreasonable or unrealistic they may sound.

In the second column, for each goal, write down all the reasons why you want to accomplish it and why it adds value or meaning to your life.

In the third column, for each goal, rate how valuable or meaningful it is to you on a scale of zero to ten, zero being the least valuable and ten being the most.

You have your life goals listed out now. Start working on them based on their importance in your life. Start ticking off the more achievable ones first so that you get the confidence boost to get the bigger stuff done.

Things I Want to Do Before I Die	**Why Is It Important for Me?**	**How Important Is This? (0-10)** **0–Not Important at All** **10–Extremely Important**
In this column, list all the things that you would like to do before you die. Be as specific as possible. It is immaterial if the to-do is impractical. If in doubt, ask yourself, "What are the things I would like/want to do if I had only one year to live?" and write down the answer.	In this column, write why those respective goals/ to-dos are important for you. If in doubt, ask yourself, "How does this add value/meaning to my life?" and write down the answer that comes to mind.	In this column, rate how important/meaningful the goals are to you, on a scale of 0-10, 0 being not meaningful/important at all and 10 being extremely important/meaningful.
For example, *I want to travel to _____.*	For example, *I have always wanted to visit the birthplace of my ancestors.*	*10*

Engage in Positive Self-Talk

Your inner critic is the biggest roadblock on your path to recovering your self-confidence. As long as you give your inner critic free rein to engage in negative self-talk, you are not going to feel confident about yourself. Engage in positive self-talk and show yourself the same compassion and empathy that you would show your best friend. The previous sections on conquering self-judgment can help you how to do this.

Discover Your Hobbies and Interests

Try out and rediscover your interest in different activities outside of your profession or academics. Ask yourself what you are passionate about. When you have an answer, add it to your list of life goals and commit to getting better at it, if it is a new pursuit. If you are interested or passionate about something, it is more probable that you will get better at it quicker and have a stronger commitment to it.

Stand Up for What You Believe In

Being confident is directly linked to standing up for what you believe in. Confident people do not hesitate to do the right thing, even if it may not be the easiest thing for them to do. Sometimes, we tend to play along with what is easier for us and compromise our values, only to end up hating ourselves for it down the line. Ask yourself what your ideal self would do. Then go ahead and do it. In the long run, you will appreciate yourself for making that choice and it will help you become more confident about your decision-making abilities.

Exercise

Exercise can not only help to keep you fit and healthy, but it can also help you manage stress, improve memory and focus, and help prevent depression. Exercise works to relieve stress by siphoning off the excess mental energy that feeds your anxiety. Make sure you get your daily workouts!

Be Brave

Everyone has secret fears and insecurities. Most often, these fears are unfounded and purely based on one's subjective feelings rather than facts. If you are afraid of failing, you need to understand that failing itself will not do much harm as much as hesitating because of fear of failure might. Failure may even serve as a learning experience. If you take a look at the lives of successful individuals, you will notice that they all had some fear of failure, but that did not stop them from going ahead and doing what they wanted to do anyway. Therein lies the secret to their confidence and success.

Honor Your Word

An important trait of confident people is that they follow through with what they say. Of course, this also means that before saying anything, they think things through to make sure they will be able to follow through with it or not. Following through with your word, without fail, adds credibility to your speech. People will respect you for it because you have proven yourself to be dependable, trustworthy, and capable of fulfilling what you commit to.

Learn to Give Zero Care to Others' Opinions of Yourself

It is very common for people to discourage others from doing what they could not achieve themselves. Do not let their rejection or their opinions bother you—whether they tell you that your goal is unreasonable, unconventional, redundant, unrealistic, or whatnot. The only opinion that should matter to you is your own. Remember that people accomplish their goals every day despite naysayers telling them that they cannot. So you do you!

Pursue Your Happiness

Always pursue the interests, hobbies, and activities that make you happy. Between work, family, and social commitments, most of us already have very little time for ourselves, so spend that time doing what you love. This is a form of self-care and will help you recharge your mental energy. Another thing to remember while in search of your inner happiness is that many unhappy people tend to sacrifice long-term happiness to fulfill their short-term desires. It is important to remember that everything you do in your life will have a trade-off. You will need to make a conscious choice every day to choose your long-term happiness over short-term joys if you want lasting happiness in your life. Remember that when the short-term costs pay off, it will well be worth it and you will feel immensely proud of your accomplishments when they do.

Keep Track of Your Improvements

One of the best ways to develop a lasting sense of self-confidence is to keep track of your improvements over time. One of the ways to do it is to fill up the following prompts and check up on yourself once a week to see if there have been any improvements.

- I have always wanted to ______________________________
- My secret fear is ______________________________
- This week I would enjoy ______________________________
- I often look forward to ______________________________
- I believe that the future, for me, holds ____________________
- I gain strength from ______________________________

- The one whom I cannot live without is ____________________
- I would never ____________________
- I felt great when ____________________
- I love it when ____________________
- I find it hard to ____________________
- I dream that one day I will ____________________
- What makes me angry is ____________________
- Smetimes, I am afraid that ____________________
- I wish this week goes ____________________
- My deepest desire is ____________________
- I thrive when ____________________
- This week, I hope to accomplish ____________________
- Sometimes I secretly do things like ____________________
- I struggle to admit ____________________

Getting Your Sense of Self-Worth Back Into Shape

Although the terms *self-confidence*, *self-esteem*, and *self-worth* are often used interchangeably, they are not technically the same. It is important to understand the basic differences between these three and work to improve these traits within each one of us.

Self-confidence is usually what we feel when we are faced with a task. It is our faith in our ability to accomplish that task successfully. Naturally, having high self-confidence means that you have great faith in your ability to achieve your goals and accomplish different tasks in life.

Having low self-confidence, by extension, means that you do not trust in your ability to finish a certain task that you have been assigned or a goal that lies in front of you.

Self-worth is how you feel about yourself, and how much value *you* think you hold, regardless of others' opinions of you. Our self-worth is determined by how much value we place upon ourselves and based upon the self-love, self-care, and self-acceptance we have for ourselves.

Self-esteem, on the other hand, is how you feel about yourself at any given moment. This is the value you place on yourself based on your accomplishments and it is largely influenced by both self-worth and self-confidence. This is because having high self-esteem requires one to have had successful accomplishments along with a sense of acknowledgment of those.

Self-esteem is more volatile than self-worth. That is because, by definition, it is indicative of how we feel at any given moment. While our self-worth may be a more stable trait, our self-esteem may keep fluctuating often, depending upon how we see ourselves as well as how others perceive us. However, self-worth is comparatively unshakeable. Having high self-worth means that you have complete faith in your abilities and you value yourself for them. It means that you accept yourself despite your weaknesses because you know what your strengths are and you are content with them. It means you are very mindful and aware of who you are as an individual and will not allow others' opinions or external events to influence that. You feel you deserve happiness and success, regardless of the roadblocks you may have to encounter. Since our self-worth depends solely on ourselves, it is a very powerful driving force in our lives and has a great impact on our successes and failures, and how we cope with them. Having high self-worth means that you will also be resilient to failures and you will be content with your successes. Because it plays such an important role in our lives, each one of us needs to develop our self-worth. However, this is not something that can be achieved overnight. It is an ongoing journey and the following steps will help you go about this:

- The first step is to get to know yourself and become more self-aware of what you are without anyone or anything else in the picture. Imagine if you lose everything overnight—all your material possessions as well as your career, relationships, and accomplishments. Now ask yourself what is it that you have left within yourself that is meaningful to you.
- The second step is to accept yourself for who you discover you are—flaws and all—after everything has been taken away from you.
- The third step is to love yourself and show yourself kindness and compassion.
- After you have learned to love yourself for who you are, it is time to move on to the fourth step and define yourself. This is where you start to form your own opinions and start becoming mindful of your emotions, regardless of what others may think.
- The fifth and final step involves taking full charge of your life. This means that you have to acknowledge your role and responsibility during everything that happens in your life..

Once you have taken complete charge of your life, that's when you have managed to develop a healthy sense of self-worth.

CHAPTER 6: EMOTIONAL REGULATION FOR COPING

Emotional regulation refers to how we process our feelings and respond in a way that is acceptable by social norms, and would be acceptable to the opposite party as well. We all experience strong emotions occasionally. Some people have an innate ability to regulate their emotions and can do so without being conscious of it. They may count up to ten, take a deep breath, talk a walk, listen to music, or meditate to self-regulate the strong feelings that they are experiencing. Once they have successfully processed them, they may respond accordingly, when they are ready to do so.

However, not everyone has this inborn ability to regulate their emotions and may need to be explicitly taught to do so. If you feel that you are being controlled by your emotions instead of you being in control of them, then read on to find out how you can take better charge of your feelings and respond to them in a way that adds value to your life, instead of detracting from it.

Is Emotional Regulation a Thing?—Importance and Dynamics

Emotions are an integral part of our lives. They play a role in how we behave, how we respond, and even how we make decisions. It is okay as long as we use our emotions and feelings to make sense of things around us. The problem arises when our emotions get the better of us and drive our behaviors in ways that may not be in our best interests. When this happens, it is important to be mindful of what we are feeling and respond accordingly, instead of behaving reactively and letting our emotions drive our behavior.

If emotional regulation does not come naturally to you, don't worry. It is a skill that can be learned by anyone, although some people may take more time to get the hang of it than others.

The first step towards regulating emotions is to recognize the situation or circumstance—whether real or imagined—that elicits the emotional response. To do this, you can ask yourself what exactly it was that happened that triggered your intense emotions. Alternatively, you could write down the sequence of events that happened in chronological order, leaving your feelings out of it, and later use this blueprint to pinpoint the exact incident that provoked the intense emotion.

The second step is to sit with the emotion and hold space for it. At this point, we usually discover that it is not the only emotion we are feeling—there may be other deep-rooted feelings behind the one we are experiencing. For example, when we get angry over someone belittling us or mocking us, it is also possible that we may be experiencing an extreme sense of shame and helplessness which, combined, has triggered the anger.

The third step is to investigate why we are experiencing all the emotions that are welling up with us. For example, if we are experiencing a sense of shame, it might do well to evaluate what's the underlying cause that is giving rise to this. Is it a low sense of self-worth? Was it a genuine error on your part? Or something else? By evaluating the core of our emotions, we are rationalizing them to know where to direct them and respond appropriately instead of being directed by them.

The last step is to respond to the emotion that was triggered. You can do this by deciding what coping mechanism works best for you to overcome the said emotion and prevent it from driving your behavior.

If you have difficulty with this process, the following activity should help make it easier for you to be more mindful of your feelings.

Trigger (What Was the Incident That Caused Me to Feel Intense Emotions?)	**What Are the Emotions That I Feel? List All That Are Applicable.**	**What Can I Do About It? (List Out the Possible Coping Mechanisms You Can Use to Respond to or Overcome This—List All That Are Applicable)**
For example, I failed to secure a contract with a client	*For example, worthless, helpless, upset, angry*	*For example: write out my feelings, talk to someone about it, etc.*

How to Use Emotional Regulation to Stay Safe from Codependency

A defining trait of codependency is an overwhelming fear of abandonment and chronic stress and anxiety resulting from this fear—that the partner may be displeased at some point for some reason and abandon them. By learning to use emotional regulation to cope with this fear and anxiety, codependents can take the edge off the emotions that drive their toxic behaviors and reclaim their independence by taking back the power in their relationships. The codependent relationship may have started as a healthy relationship before the balance of power slowly shifted in favor of one partner, or it could have been a dysfunctional dynamic from the get-go. Either way, codependents need to regulate their fear and stress if they want to take charge of their lives and break free from the toxic patterns that will otherwise follow them through all their relationships.

Avoiding Getting Sucked into Another Codependent Relationship

Since you now have the tools to free yourself from your current codependent tendencies—either by way of reworking your behavioral patterns and growing within the relationship or by breaking free from the relationship that was holding you down—the next question on your mind may be, "How do I avoid getting trapped in another codependent relationship or pattern?" That is a very valid question. Not only because people who choose to grow out of their codependent patterns within their relationship tend to relapse into their old habits, but also because codependents who break up with their toxic partners tend to seek new relationships that repeat similar patterns.

The way to avoid getting sucked into another codependent relationship is to first learn about codependency, recognize your role in the codependency cycle, and course-correct to replace codependent habits and behaviors with healthier ones.

Step 1: Understanding Codependency in Your Personal Context

The first step to not repeating codependent patterns is to not just understand codependency in general, but also recognize how it plays out in your personal life. Do you find yourself trying to control or being controlled? Are you the kind of person who needs your partner to save you every time you face a minor hiccup in life or are you the one playing the hero? Are you the one who falls in love way too easily and ends up getting hurt or do you push people away even when they fit your needs perfectly? Do you blame your partner for your unhappy life or do you blame yourself for the imagined hurts that you have caused your partner?

It is important to understand that codependency does not play out the same way for any two people, or even for the same person in two different relationships. Understanding how codependency is crippling your happiness is half the job done. If you do this right, the rest of the puzzle pieces will fall into place on their own.

Step 2: Reevaluate Your Codependent Expectations

Once you have understood your personal codependent patterns, it is important to understand where your codependent behavior and expectations stem from. The roots of codependency are intricate and untangling them requires a lot of introspection and self-work. Often, there isn't just one thing that has caused someone to develop codependent behavior. It is often a mix of various factors forming a unique cocktail that translates into the individual's signature behavioral pattern—which is why I stated in the previous step that codependency does not unfold the same way for two people.

Ask yourself if what you expect from your partner stems from your past emotions and relationships, the structure of the family that you were raised in, or social pressures. Once you have realized this, ask yourself how important it is for you to uphold these expectations. Are you going to face practical losses or pushback if your expectations are not met? Chances are, your sense of loss is more imagined than realistic—such is the nature of codependency. Once you unpack your expectations and start to view them pragmatically, you can identify where your unhealthy behavior stems from.

Step 3: Set Boundaries

Boundaries provide structure to a relationship, and without structure, a relationship is chaotic. To be able to set strong boundaries, you need to first understand yourself and your core values—what your expectations, needs, and limits of giving are in a relationship. Once you understand this, you need to be able to set limits and convey them. However, don't expect people to change overnight, and start respecting your boundaries without pushback. Learn to be assertive and focus on changing yourself and focusing your energy where it matters rather than trying to change others to match your expectations. Finally, check in with yourself and your feelings every day. By holding space for yourself and your feelings, you will be more mindful of what you feel and why you feel it, and this can help you reassess and readjust your boundaries as needed.

Step 4: Do Not Try to Rescue or Control

At the core of codependency is essentially a savior complex that makes one believe that they are only worthy of love if they are either saving someone from impending doom, fixing up—with their impeccable damage control skills—a disaster that has already struck, or controlling a person to save them from their own toxicity. It is important to remember that it is not your job to foresee or mind-read what they need and provide it to them. No one can ever truly know what another person needs—only they can. This is very important to keep in mind on the path to codependency recovery. You cannot fix a person who does not want to be fixed, you cannot save a person who does not want to be saved, and you cannot control anyone, except yourself.

Step 5: Remember Your Own Value

Always remember that any relationship you have has to add value to your already fulfilling life. It should not be the reason you find your life fulfilling. People come and people go. Your life is your journey and there will be certain phases that you will need to undertake alone. When you are the only person who is there for you, make sure that you are in good company. Never stop caring and loving yourself for who you are. Only when you can add value to your life, will you be able to add value to another's, as well as understand the value that a partner is adding to yours.

How to Avoid Any Other Kind of Toxic Relationship

One way to avoid toxic relationships is by being proactively mindful of the kind of people you enter into relationships with at an early stage. Before you get all moon-eyed over Mr./Miss Toxic, learn to identify their red flags and eliminate anyone who does not seem to be a good match for you. A red flag need not just be verbal or emotional abuse. If you feel that your values do not align, that could be a potential red flag too. When you show up as your authentic self, your partner needs to show up the same way for you. Don't be afraid to speak your truth and assert your reality and your feelings as you experience them. Any partner who rejects you or is dismissive of your reality can be shown the door.

Don't take setbacks in your romantic life personally. Take your past relationships as learning experiences and they will help you grow into a better individual. When you renew your search, make sure you are an individual who has a more secure attachment style than the past you. Although no one can have a 100% secure attachment style, you can always do the work to move closer to being a securely attached individual to experience healthier relationships.

If you are already in a relationship, then commit to being mindful of your emotional health while you are in it and be intentional about keeping toxicity out of it. Relationships can only work if both partners are intentional about making it work. Learn to show gestures of love to your partner the way they like to be loved rather than the way you do. Instinctively, we love our partners the way we would like to be shown love. For example, if you are a gifts person, you may shower your partner with gifts, when all they want from you is a few moments to spend their time with. Learn to accept your differences in the way you show and receive love and find a middle ground that works for both of you. Make time for each other regularly, have fun together, and appreciate the little joys that your relationship brings you. Couples that have fun together, stay together. Also, when things are not feeling all that good, don't hesitate to communicate them with your partner. Good communication is the key to a good relationship.

PART 3:

STAYING FREE

CHAPTER 7: GOOD OLD BOUNDARIES

As mentioned earlier, boundaries are the cornerstone of healthy relationships. They provide structure to relationships, regardless of the kind of relationship—romantic, familial, or platonic. Relationships that lack structure break down into toxic, dysfunctional versions of themselves. Since boundaries are so important, let us find out what they are and how to establish them for improving the quality of our relationships.

What Are Boundaries?

Boundaries are the imaginary lines that we draw to mark our physical, mental, and emotional space as being separate and autonomous, from that of anyone else's. Boundaries are also an indicator to people of what we will tolerate and what we will not. If you have not yet established boundaries, then it is likely that you have often found yourself being taken advantage of—which is why boundaries are necessary. In the words of Henry Ford,

> *"Givers have to set limits because the takers rarely do."*
>
> **(Svoboda, 2021)**

Imagine you own a house with a front lawn that has a garden. If you do not put up a fence, soon you may have your neighbors, their children, or their pets, walking all over your lawn, picking your flowers, or messing it up in general. However, if you look at the situation rationally, it was you who did not put up a tangible boundary to mark your real estate; you who did not demarcate your property as being off-limits, effectively allowing them to simply come in and run amok on your grounds.

Similarly, if you do not establish clear and firm boundaries pertaining to your personal space, time, or possessions, you may find that soon, people will not hesitate to come and trample all over you. However, chances are that if you are not assertive enough to state your boundaries from the get-go, you probably are also not assertive enough to ask them to stop treating you like a doormat until you are completely drained and have reached a breaking point. If you have experienced that breaking point once, you know it's not pretty and you certainly do not want to experience emotional burnout ever again. This is why we need boundaries.

Boundaries allow us to be true to ourselves and live in alignment with our ideals and goals. They allow us to follow our principles and values without having to compromise them for the sake of pleasing someone else. They are also a basic form of self-care. Even if you don't have time to go to that luxury getaway and recharge yourself, you will need to set some boundaries with everyone around you so that you can rest and recoup in the comfort of your home, at the very least. They keep you from stretching yourself too thin for the other party, be it your family, friends, or workplace. They also help you set realistic expectations with the said opposite party so that they know what they can ask of you and what they cannot. Boundaries help create your own safe space where you can keep out anything that seeks to disturb your physical, mental, or emotional security.

Who Do You Need to Set Boundaries With?

Boundaries are needed in all relationships. While some relationships have their unspoken boundaries, sometimes some people can be clueless and test boundaries. It is usually with such individuals that you will need to set firm boundaries. On the other hand, some people will disrespect your boundaries—even after you have stated them clearly—and give you pushback for the same. In such cases, you will need to restate and reinforce your boundaries and state clear consequences that you are willing to follow through with, should your boundary be violated again. Fundamentally, you will need to set boundaries with any person who makes you uncomfortable and you will need to stand your ground on the fact that you are not okay with their behavior.

Sometimes, however, it turns out that we are the toxic ones and in such cases, we may need to set firm boundaries for ourselves to change the way we react to our social stimuli. Some of the signs that you need to have stronger boundaries for yourself are given below.

- If you feel that you are perpetually being taken for granted or taken advantage of—whether it be physically, emotionally, mentally, or financially.
- When you find that your resources are being drained, such that there isn't even enough left for yourself, you need to start asking yourself what boundaries you need to set for yourself that will give you the power to prevent others from doing this to you.
- If you have difficulty refusing people and you keep saying "yes" even if you have to make up for it at the expense of your well-being.

- If you are constantly neglecting your own needs because you are afraid to speak up for yourself since you fear it may cause conflict and hence allow others to have their way at all times.
- You allow others to disrespect you—whether it is in the form of passing hurtful or sarcastic comments, mocking or belittling you—instead of taking a stand for yourself.
- You fear being abandoned so you make do with whatever little you receive in a relationship, even if, sometimes, you feel like you are receiving nothing in return at all.
- Making everyone around you happy has become very important to you and you are desperate to win everyone's approval.
- If you engage in disrespectful behaviors that are hurting others, or someone has informed you that they have been hurt by your behavior.
- If you are flirting with individuals who are already in relationships or if you are flirting even when you are in a committed relationship even though you will most definitely end up hurting your partner.
- When you believe that you are entitled to get what you want, by hook or by crook, because you believe the rules don't apply to you.

Although engaging in the above behaviors might feel like "it works" for you at the moment, all the above are toxic, self-sabotaging behaviors that will end up hurting you down the line. It is better to identify them and learn to set boundaries for yourself before you find yourself experiencing the physical or mental drain that such behaviors and belief patterns can cause.

Why Boundaries Will Never Go Out of Fashion

Imagine if your partner constantly makes bad financial decisions and ends up incurring debts that they have no way of paying off. What happens if your partner does not pay off this debt? Do they go to prison or lose their job or their house? Thinking of the devastating consequences, you offer to help out your partner with their debts, but in a few months, you find that they have incurred a new set of debts to pay off and come to you for help.

Imagine if you have taken time off for your friend from your busy schedule and decided to meet up at a local cafe halfway between where you both live. Your friend insists that you meet up closer to where they live and you accept their idea because you are excited to meet them after such a long time. Since you have engagements to get back to, you let them know that you have only a couple of hours that you can spend with them. Now imagine if your friend turns up late or does not turn up at all.

Imagine if you have a roommate that you share an apartment with, and they have an annoying habit of entering your bedroom without your permission and going through your stuff or even borrowing it sometimes. You often end up having to look for your own stuff in your room because it is missing since they have borrowed it without informing you beforehand or because they have put it back in your room but out of the original place that they took it from.

In all of the above situations, your boundaries are being violated. Many people find themselves in similar situations and allow the boundary violations to continue.

In the first scenario, they may continue to enable their partner because they fear that their partner may leave them if they do not keep compensating for their partner's financial situation.

In the second, although their time is being disrespected, they may let it slide because they are afraid of creating conflict in a long-standing friendship.

In the third scenario, although their personal space is being violated, and they may feel annoyed or upset, they may let it slide because they have never been taught to assert boundaries respectfully and fear coming across as aggressive.

Learning to assert boundaries is very important for any individual who seeks to pursue a positive mindset and emotionally healthy relationships. Boundaries allow us to maintain and improve our sense of self-esteem and self-worth.

They allow us to progress through relationships at our own pace—from sharing information to becoming intimate, they allow us to keep our personal and emotional space safe. They prevent a lopsided power imbalance in a relationship and allow both parties to share an equal partnership, responsibility, and power.

They allow us to be assertive and behave in alignment with our inner thoughts and feelings so that we can show up as our authentic selves for others, say "yes" only when we are in full honest agreement, and say "no" when we feel uncomfortable with anything, as well as respect other people for the differences they may have with us.

They also grant us autonomy and help keep our sense of self and our identity separate from others.

They prevent us from building our identity around another person and help us understand that our thoughts, opinions, feelings, and emotions are unique and separate from anyone else's.

Lastly, they empower us to make our own decisions and take responsibility for our lives.

Kinds of Boundaries to Set

There are different kinds of boundaries that we may need to establish based on the circumstances, but most of them fall into one of the following categories:

Physical Boundaries

Physical boundaries safeguard our physical space and our bodies. Some of the common physical boundaries are our right not to be touched in ways that make us feel uncomfortable, our right to privacy, and our right to take care of ourselves via healthy eating and getting a good rest. They define how close someone can get to us and what kind of physical touch—if any—will be tolerated, where and how much privacy we require, and how others can behave in our personal space.

For example, when you ask not to be disturbed during certain hours because you need your rest or when you refuse to eat food that contains something you are allergic to, you are setting a physical boundary.

Emotional Boundaries

Emotional boundaries safeguard our emotional autonomy and our right not to have our feelings dismissed or belittled. Emotional boundaries help us separate our feelings from those of others so that we are not influenced by others' emotional states. They also help separate emotional responsibilities so that, while we are responsible for regulating our own emotions, we are not responsible for how others feel. They also help us safeguard our emotional security by allowing us to share only the feelings that we may be comfortable with.

For example, when someone at your workplace asks you to talk about your personal life and you refuse, or when someone at home has an emotional outburst of grief and you take a walk outside to prevent their emotional state from affecting your own, you are setting emotional boundaries.

Sexual Boundaries

Sexual boundaries safeguard our right to sexual consent, preference, privacy, and contraception usage. Sexual boundaries define what our sexual preferences are; what, when, and with whom we consent to have sex; our right to use contraception and knowledge of our partner's usage of the same; and our right to protection of our privacy and our intimate details.

For example, when you refuse to have sex on the first date or when you clarify to your partner to use contraceptives if you are to have sex, then you are exercising sexual boundaries.

Time Boundaries

Time boundaries safeguard our time and define how, with whom, and how much of our time we spend. They prevent us from wasting time with people who do not add any value to our lives or spending it with people who do not respect our time, as well as help us avoid being physically burnt out.

For example, when you inform your workplace that you will spend your weekends with your family and that you will respond to work emails only on business days, you are setting a time boundary.

Intellectual or Mental Boundaries

Intellectual boundaries safeguard our rights to express our thoughts, opinions, and ideas without fear of being dismissed or belittled. They are defined by mutual respect when exchanging ideas and willingness to engage in respectful dialogue despite any differences that may arise.

For example, if you agree to disagree with a friend who has different political opinions, or express to them that you are not comfortable discussing political opinions because it is affecting your relationship, then you are exercising intellectual boundaries.

Material or Financial Boundaries

Material boundaries safeguard our possessions such as our homes, belongings, and money. They define how we prefer to share, lend, or give away our possessions and how we expect our things to be treated if we are sharing them or when we expect them to be returned if we are lending them.

For example, if you refuse to bail out a person from debt but you are ready to refer them to a job so they can earn and pay off the loan on their own, you are exercising your material boundaries. Such boundaries also come into play if you clarify when you want your things back, if someone asks to borrow them, or if you refuse to lend them out for any reason.

Spiritual or Religious Boundaries

Spiritual boundaries safeguard your right to believe and worship what you wish, as well as practice your spiritual or religious beliefs.

For example, if you refuse to go to church with your partner but you do not stop them from practicing their own faith, you would be exercising religious boundaries.

How to Set Boundaries to Overcome Codependency

Now that you have understood the different kinds of boundaries, what they look like, and when and why they are needed, it is time to learn how to set boundaries and assert them to have healthier relationships. The following process can help you assert your boundaries without feeling guilty:

1. The first step is to think about why you want to establish a certain boundary. With whom do you want to establish this boundary? Why do you want to set a boundary with them? Has their behavior ever caused you discomfort or disturbed you in any way? If so, how? Think of your values and how anyone may have violated or caused you to violate these. What was their behavior at the time?

2. Think about what kind of boundary you are going to set and what you hope to accomplish by establishing it. Use your values as the yardstick to compare how you would want to make required changes so that your behavior or your actions align with your internal compass.

3. Next, decide how you will assert that boundary and when you will choose to do so. Expect there to be pushback and go in with the expectation that not everyone is going to accept your boundaries and feel better about it. Learn to speak your mind in clear, firm, and concise terms, leaving no room for doubt or gray areas.

4. Finally, decide upon the consequences you are willing to enforce if your boundaries are violated. Make sure that the consequences are not simply empty threats, but something that you can readily enforce. Otherwise, your entire assertion of boundaries loses its value.

The following activity should make it easy for you, should you have difficulty understanding how to set boundaries.

The Person I Feel Uncomfortable/Upset/Hurt With	
What Behavior of Theirs Makes Me Uncomfortable/Upset/Hurt?	
Kind of Boundary I Need to Set (Physical/ Emotional/ Financial/ Sexual/ Time-Bound/ Moral etc.)	
What Are the Limits of This Boundary—What Is Acceptable to Me and What Is Not?	
What Is the Consequence That I Am Willing to Follow Through with if This Boundary Is Violated?	

CHAPTER 8: INTERDEPENDENT RELATIONSHIPS THAT WORK

We have explored unhealthy relationships and how to deal with them in detail. However, all this exploration is incomplete if one does not understand what a healthy relationship looks like and what it constitutes. If one has to truly move on from codependency, one must be aware of how to avoid going to the other extreme of over-independence, but instead, work on cultivating a healthy interdependence where both partners share equal effort and responsibility in the relationship.

Dangers of Over-Independence

Have you ever heard anyone say, "I am perfectly fine being single," "I am better off without a man/woman in my life," "Relationships are way too complicated and just not worth the trouble," or "What do I need a man/woman for? I'm doing just fine on my own?" Well, do not believe them or follow their example because it is a lie. It is just as much a lie as codependency. Except it is worse because people who are in codependent relationships fall into the trap subconsciously, but people who follow this pattern of over-independence or hyper-independence have, sadly, *chosen* to make their lives worse. It is a choice that is misguided and damaging to their emotional and physical well-being, more than they can possibly realize.

Human beings have evolved to form two major attachments as adults. The first is to our parent(s) and the second is to our romantic partner. These two attachments are more intricately linked than we realize. We have already seen how having an emotionally unavailable parent can affect our relationships going forward, causing insecure attachment, codependency, and a myriad of other relationship and mental health issues. One possible cause of hyper-independence is also when we haven't had our needs met as a child and been parentified—being burdened with taking on the responsibility that should have been fulfilled by an adult—because that is when we have become so used to doing things on our own that it has gone on to become the norm. We then find it difficult to ask for help, even when we need it.

Of course, no one chooses to have their heart broken or be left alone to fend for themselves. However, as an adult, it is every individual's responsibility to themselves to heal from the wounds that they carry for the sake of their well-being going forward. This is something we all owe to ourselves. We cannot choose the hurt that others cause us but we can choose to heal from it and lead fuller lives. We can choose to be gentle with ourselves and give ourselves the love and companionship that we deserve—the partner that we deserve. We owe it to ourselves to improve our emotional and mental health to become worthy of that person when they come along. The following activity can help you take your first step forward, toward a healthier mindset:

Step 1: Write down one small way that someone else can show up for you today and have a go at it. It does not have to be a huge deal. It could just be something as simple as asking your partner to help you with the dishes or laundry.

Step 2: Now write down how it felt to ask something of them. What was it like for you before you asked them? How did they respond—did they accept? What was it like after they responded?

Interdependence, the Opposite of Codependency

Many individuals recover from codependency only to land up in a state of hyper-independence. However, it is important to remember that neither approach is healthy and sustainable for your well-being in the long run. The key is to develop a healthy and sustainable relationship where both partners can share happiness and joy as equals.

Interdependence is a choice between two emotionally healthy individuals to come together and form a couple. Each of them finds that they have their own areas of interest that fulfill them as well as common interests as a couple in the relationships that unite them and bring them closer. Both of them love and support each other while simultaneously respecting the other's boundaries.

Interdependent relationships are characterized by clearly defined boundaries between the partners that are respected by them both; autonomy of opinions, thoughts, beliefs, emotions, and goals, while including your partner; a sense of self-awareness and having one's identity defined individually as a person, and not just as being one half of a couple; viewing their relationships as a work in progress in which both of them continuously make an effort to communicate empathetically and effectively, and respect each other; and where both of them feel safe in the relationship and trust their ability to strengthen the relationship and work together to resolve the issues that come with being in a relationship.

The Importance of Forming Healthy Relationships

Healthy relationships ensure that we have better mental health. A healthy mind leads to a healthier body. Let us explore some of the benefits of having a healthy relationship.

Reduces Stress

Studies indicate that having a healthy committed relationship or strong friendship that provides social and emotional support can help to reduce stress levels. Research also indicates that it has a positive effect on our biological systems and helps to regulate blood pressure and strengthen our immune system. Conversely, not having a good social support system has been correlated to health deterioration, which is almost equal to smoking 15 cigarettes a day. (Acenda Integrated Health, 2019)

Healing Touch

They say that love hurts but a healthy form of love heals, rather than hurts. Research suggests that "patients, with long-term partners, who have undergone heart surgery are three times more likely to survive the first three months after surgery than patients who are single" (Northwestern Medicine Staff, 2017). Patients who have long-term partners and are in committed relationships have also been reported as having more faith in their ability to handle post-surgery trauma and have comparatively less anxiety about the surgical procedure. This shows that a little emotional support can go a long way to helping someone heal and recover from illness.

Healthier Habits

Healthier relationships encourage people to pursue a healthier lifestyle and integrate healthier habits into their routines. If you have a partner, friend, or family member who encourages you to eat healthily, exercise, avoid smoking, etc, you are likelier to model your behavior after their support and encouragement since we all find it easier to integrate healthier behaviors if everyone around us is doing the same.

Sense of Purpose

Having healthy relationships can increase your sense of self-worth, boost your self-confidence and improve your sense of belonging. Having a friend or partner who is there for you no matter what can improve your sense of purpose in life and make you feel like you are adding value to their lives, while at the same time adding value to yours.

Increases Longevity

Research has linked a better social life to an increase in longevity (Northwestern Medicine Staff, 2017). This is a given considering that healthier relationships have enormous health benefits and improve emotional health to a great degree. Although some people, especially introverts, may feel more comfortable spending more time alone, they need social interactions too, and having even very few close but strong friendships—even if it is just one or two friends—can compensate for their desire to avoid social situations.

It's Okay to Need Help

We live in a world that glorifies independence and individuality and it is easy to lose track. If you take it a tad bit extreme, you might start treading on the path of hyper-independence.

It is alright to look for a partner and look to them for emotional support. It is alright to have a friend or a social support system to fall back on when the going gets tough and ask for help. So why are you still hesitant?

Are you under the impression that you are a burden to those whom you are asking for help from? Well, research indicates that "we are appreciated and cared for more than we realize, and when asked if they perceived a peer positively or negatively, the adjectives that people used to characterize others were quite positive" (Funder, 1980; TD Jakes, 2022). Remember that people who are loved have a special place in our hearts and that works the other way around as well. So, if you are wondering if someone may find it offensive or bothersome if you ask for help, remember that they don't, and reach out to the person in question because chances are that they may be more welcoming than you imagine them to be.

If you, instead, feel a sense of vulnerability and weakness by asking for help, remind yourself that asking for help does not make you weak. You are strong for doing all that you did on your own and there are times when you will have to take a break and allow others to support you. You do not lose your power by asking for help.

If you still feel a sense of obligation after receiving help, then go ahead and pay it forward. This will help you find a sense of purpose and fulfillment. Remember that asking for help does not make you any less of a person, nor does it reduce your power. Instead, it empowers you to become a better person.

How to Grow and Cultivate Healthy Relationships with Genuinely Helpful People

Nurturing healthy relationships requires you to break your old unhealthy habits and behavior patterns and cultivate new ones in their stead. Some of the habits and patterns you will need to cultivate are listed below.

Authenticity

Any healthy relationship requires that you be open and honest from the get-go. That does not mean that you overshare all the information you have about yourself—you can, of course, take time to share information that you are comfortable with—but the key is to avoid pretending to be or turning into the person you think that the opposite party will like.

Empathy

Empathy is the ability to put yourself in someone's shoes and relate to them and validate their experiences without making it all about yourself.

Thoughtfulness

Relationships require you to be thoughtful and mindful of each other. This means that you have to be aware of each other's needs and desires, and put in a conscious effort to fulfill them to the best of your abilities. You can do this by being mindful of what makes your partner happy and showing them love in ways that work for them rather than ways that work for you.

Presence

Relationships require you to be present for your partner. This does not just mean physical presence. It also means that you need to be 100% present and available for them emotionally and mentally when you spend time with them. You can do this by putting away your devices, taking a break and disconnecting from work while you are with them, and giving them your fu.ll attention when they are with you. Focusing on what they say and giving them your undivided attention by making eye contact can strengthen the bond between you.

Reliability

Reliability and dependability are important traits if you want to sustain healthy relationships. In any relationship, you will need the other party to follow through on what they say. You need to be able to trust them and know that when they say they are going to do something they will. Although we may inevitably fail to keep our commitments from time to time, as long as we put effort and communicate openly about the setbacks we have faced that have prevented us from keeping our word, there will likely be forgiveness and trust still intact in the relationship.

Communication

Good communication is the cornerstone of any relationship, be it familial, platonic, romantic, or professional. However, it becomes very important for partners to learn to communicate with each other effectively because of the sheer amount of time they spend together and the number of life issues they will need to resolve together.

Compromise

All relationships involve give and take. A healthy relationship requires both partners to be willing to meet each other halfway. Since no two individuals are the same, it is normal for differences to arise and when differences arise, both parties must come together to find a common ground that works for them both.

Boundaries

Boundaries are an essential part of any relationship. Just as it is important to establish boundaries, it is equally important to respect the boundaries of one's partner, if the relationship has to thrive, even if their boundaries are different from yours. One needs to understand that just as no two individuals are completely alike, their sense of boundaries may not be the same either. Accepting the differences and working to make those differences work is an essential skill to maintain and sustain long-term relationships.

Gratitude

All relationships experience ups and downs and no relationship is perfect. Both partners will experience both good times and not-so-happy times in their relationship. It is important to cherish the happier moments in the relationship and have the maturity to let go of the less happy ones to keep the relationship going.

CONCLUSION

When you began reading this book, you wanted to learn how to escape from codependency and reclaim your power so that you can stop feeling helpless and out of control of your life. In this book, you have now learned about what a codependent relationship looks like and the different parties in a codependent relationship, why codependent relationships are unhealthy and difficult to get out of, the codependency enablers, who codependents attract and who they are attracted to, the importance of prioritizing yourself, why narcissists are usually drawn to codependents, what causes fear of abandonment and codependency, and how to overcome the fear of abandonment.

You've learned how to build self-worth and self-confidence to improve your relationships, how to use emotional regulation against codependency, how to avoid toxic relationships, what boundaries are and how to establish and maintain boundaries, what hyper-dependency is and why it is unhealthy. You've learned about codependent versus interdependent relationships, and finally how to form and maintain healthy interdependent relationships.

Now that you have all the tools to overcome your codependency, go out there and use them to find your freedom. Remember that you deserve to be loved and seen for who you are so claim your right and beat your codependency demons out of your life!

If you have enjoyed reading this book, please leave your review on Amazon and be sure to recommend it to your friends who may be facing similar struggles.

THANK YOU

Thank you so much for purchasing this book.

You could have picked from dozens of other books about codependency, but you took a chance and chose this one.

So THANK YOU for getting this book and for reading it all the way to the end.

Before you go, I wanted to ask you for one small favor. **Could you please consider posting a review on Amazon? Posting a review is the best and easiest way to support the work of independent authors like me.**

Your feedback will also help me to keep writing the kind of books that will help you get the results you want. It would mean a lot to me to hear from you.

>> **Leave a review on Amazon US** <<

>> **Leave a review on Amazon UK** <<

REFERENCES

A Conscious Rethink. (2016, August 24). *Codependency Vs Caring: Differentiating Between The Harmful And The Helpful.* A Conscious Rethink. https://www.aconsciousrethink.com/3858/codependency-vs-caring-differentiating-harmful-helpful/

A Little Dose of Happy. (2022, August 15). *9 Tips For Cultivating Relationships That Last - a little dose of happy.* A Little Dose of Happy. https://aldohappy.com/cultivating-relationships

Acenda Integrated Health. (2019, August 3). *4 Benefits of Healthy Relationships.* Acenda. https://acendahealth.org/4-benefits-of-healthy-relationships/

Ackerman, C. E. (2019, June 19). *18 Self-Esteem Worksheets and Activities for Teens and Adults (+PDFs).* PositivePsychology.com. https://positivepsychology.com/self-esteem-worksheets/

Alyssa. (2019, November 25). *Codependency: Enabling vs. Supportive Behavior.* Banyan Treatment Center. https://www.banyantreatmentcenter.com/2019/11/25/codependency-enabling-vs-supportive-behavior/

Anderson, S. (2015, April 3). *How to Overcome Fear of Abandonment: 7 Dos and 10 Don'ts*. HuffPost. https://www.huffpost.com/entry/how-to-overcome-fear-of-a_b_6988748/amp

Annie Highwater. (n.d.). *Codependency, the cycle of low self-worth – anniehighwater*. Annie Highwater. Retrieved November 10, 2022, from http://anniehighwater.com/codependency-the-cycle-of-low-self-worth/

Applebury, G. (2020, August 13). *6 Dysfunctional Family Roles and Their Characteristics*. LoveToKnow. https://family.lovetoknow.com/about-family-values/6-dysfunctional-family-roles-their-characteristics

Araminta. (2021, January 8). *The Subtle Effects of Trauma: People Pleasing*. Khiron Clinics. https://khironclinics.com/blog/people-pleasing/#:~:text=Emotional%20Responses%20Related%20to%20Fawning%2FPeople%2DPleasing&text=Common%20challenges%20and%20emotions%20faced

Beau, A. (2021, October 8). *6 Mantras to Help You Prioritize Yourself and Your Needs*. Shine. https://advice.theshineapp.com/articles/6-mantras-to-help-you-prioritize-yourself-and-your-needs/

Belle, E. (2020, May 22). *Codependency: How Emotional Neglect Turns Us Into People-Pleasers*. Healthline. https://www.healthline.com/health/mental-health/codependency-and-attachment-trauma

Berry, J. (2017, October 31). *Codependent relationships: Symptoms, warning signs, and behavior*. Medical News Today. https://www.medicalnewstoday.com/articles/319873#signs-and-symptoms-of-codependency

Boyd, A. (2022, October 4). *Keep Healthy Relationships 101: How To Stop Being Codependent | Discover How To Stop Being Codependent Today | BetterHelp*. Better Help. https://www.betterhelp.com/advice/how-to/healthy-relationships-101-how-to-stop-being-codependent/

Brazier, Y., & Sissons, B. (2020, August 3). *Narcissistic personality disorder: Symptoms, diagnosis, and treatment*. Www.medicalnewstoday.com. https://www.medicalnewstoday.com/articles/9741#diagnosis

Breen, P. (2020, February 24). *What is Codependency and Why is it Dangerous?* Grotto Network. https://grottonetwork.com/navigate-life/relationships/is-codependency-bad/

Bridges, F. (2017, July 21). *10 Ways To Build Confidence*. Forbes. https://www.forbes.com/sites/francesbridges/2017/07/21/10-ways-to-build-confidence/?sh=1ff6ad123c59

Brooten-Brooks, M. C. (2022, January 24). *How to Set Healthy Boundaries*. Verywell Health. https://www.verywellhealth.com/setting-boundaries-5208802

Campbell, L. (2021, June 8). *Personal Boundaries: Types and How to Set Them*. Psych Central. https://psychcentral.com/lib/what-are-personal-boundaries-how-do-i-get-some

Carter, L. (2021, June 21). *"You Can't Pour From an Empty Cup": Why Self-Care Isn't Selfish – Modern Minds.* Modern Minds. https://modern-minds.com/you-cant-pour-from-an-empty-cup-why-self-care-isnt-selfish/#:~:text=Have%20you%20ever%20heard%20the

Cleveland Clinic. (2022, January 28). *10 Signs You're in a Codependent Relationship.* Cleveland Clinic. https://health.clevelandclinic.org/codependent-relationship-signs/

Dance, M. (2021, October 21). *The Root Cause of Codependency and How to Break the Cycle.* Mary Ellen Dance. https://pittsfordtherapy.com/the-root-cause-of-codependency-and-how-to-break-the-cycle/

Davin, Dr. K. (2022, May 15). *How to Become Less Codependent in Your Relationship.* Dr. Kristin Davin, Psy.D. https://reflectionsfromacrossthecouch.com/blog/how-to-become-less-codependent-in-your-relationship

Donnelly, M. (2017, February 28). *It's Okay To Ask For Help, You Know.* Thought Catalog. https://thoughtcatalog.com/marisa-donnelly/2017/02/its-okay-to-ask-for-help-you-know/

Earnshaw, E. (2019, July 20). *6 Types of boundaries you deserve to have (and how to maintain them).* MindBodyGreen. https://www.mindbodygreen.com/articles/six-types-of-boundaries-and-what-healthy-boundaries-look-like-for-each

Fellizar, K. (2018, December 3). *How to Stop Being Codependent: Moving Past Codependency | Zencare.* The Couch: A Therapy & Mental Wellness Blog. https://blog.zencare.co/how-to-stop-being-codependent/amp/

Finch, S. D. (2019, September 30). *7 Subtle Signs Your Trauma Response Is People-Pleasing*. Healthline. https://www.healthline.com/health/mental-health/7-subtle-signs-your-trauma-response-is-people-pleasing

Firestone, L. (2017, August 17). *The Unselfish Art of Prioritizing Yourself | Psychology Today*. Psychology Today. https://www.psychologytoday.com/us/blog/compassion-matters/201708/the-unselfish-art-prioritizing-yourself?amp

Fishman, R. (2018, April 16). *7 Ways to Respond to Self-Judgment - Renée Fishman*. My Meadow Report. https://mymeadowreport.com/reneefishman/2018/7-ways-to-respond-to-self-judgment/

Fleming, J. (2020, December 2). *You can't pour from an empty cup...* Direction Psychology. https://www.directionpsychology.com/article/you-cant-pour-from-an-empty-cup/

Fort Behavioral Health. (2020, January 24). *9 Warning Signs of a Codependent Relationship*. Fort Behavioral Health. https://www.fortbehavioral.com/addiction-recovery-blog/9-warning-signs-of-a-codependent-relationship/

Fritscher, L. (2019). *Why Some People Experience a Fear of Abandonment*. Verywell Mind. https://www.verywellmind.com/fear-of-abandonment-2671741

Funder, D. C. (1980). On seeing ourselves as others see us: Self-other agreement and discrepancy in personality ratings. *Journal of Personality*, *48*(4), 473–493. https://doi.org/10.1111/j.1467-6494.1980.tb02380.x

Gaba, S. (2019a, January 31). *Escaping the Codependent-Narcissist Trap.* Wake up Recovery. https://wakeuprecovery.com/escaping-the-codependent-narcissist-trap/

Gaba, S. (2019b, August 4). *Boundaries and the Dance of the Codependent | Psychology Today.* Psychology Today. https://www.psychologytoday.com/us/blog/addiction-and-recovery/201908/boundaries-and-the-dance-the-codependent?amp

Gaba, S. (2019c, September 4). *Why Codependents Attract Narcissists | Psychology Today.* Psychology Today. https://www.psychologytoday.com/intl/blog/addiction-and-recovery/201909/why-codependents-attract-narcissists?amp

Gilbert, B. (2020, July 16). *Do You Have a Codependent Personality? | Everyday Health.* EverydayHealth.com. https://www.everydayhealth.com/emotional-health/do-you-have-a-codependent-personality.aspx

Gilmour, P., & Gulla, E. (2022, January 20). *Are you in an unhealthy codependent relationship? These are the signs to look out for.* Cosmopolitan. https://www.cosmopolitan.com/uk/love-sex/relationships/a13985366/codependency-relationship-signs/

Glass, L. J. (2020, September 1). *Codependents & Boundaries: Why Do They Struggle?* PIVOT. https://www.lovetopivot.com/what-cause-triggers-codependency-boundaries-recovery-coaching/

Good Therapy. (2009, September 15). *Fear of Abandonment Issues and Therapy Treatment.* Good Therapy. https://www.goodtherapy.org/learn-about-therapy/issues/abandonment

Gunther, R., Sherman, A., Patterson, A., & Schinke, K. (2020, February 4). *How To Know If I am in a Codependent Relationship - 4 Experts Share Totally Awesome Insights - Deep Soulful Love.* Deep Soulful Love. https://deepsoulfullove.com/how-to-know-if-i-am-in-a-codependent-relationship/

Haas, S. B. (2016, September 28). *Self-Care 101: You Can't Pour From an Empty Cup | Psychology Today.* Www.psychologytoday.com. https://www.psychologytoday.com/us/blog/prescriptions-life/201609/self-care-101-you-can-t-pour-empty-cup?amp

Happe, M. (2011, August 12). *The Relationship between Narcissism and Codependency - Relationship Problems ?EUR" Tools to Build and Maintain a Healthy Marriage.* MentalHelp.net. https://www.mentalhelp.net/blogs/the-relationship-between-narcissism-and-codependency/

Haskell, E. F. (2021, October 10). *Dr. Erin Podcast: The Truth About Narcissism and Codependency Relationships.* Erinfallhaskell.libsyn.com. https://erinfallhaskell.libsyn.com/the-truth-about-narcissism-and-codependency-relationships

Health Direct. (n.d.). *Building and maintaining healthy relationships.* Www.healthdirect.gov.au. https://www.healthdirect.gov.au/amp/article/building-and-maintaining-healthy-relationships

Horsfall, A. (2017, November 7). *When Being a Pushover Becomes a Problem | HealthyPlace.* Healthy Place. https://www.healthyplace.com/blogs/toughtimes/2017/11/when-being-a-pushover-becomes-a-problem

Howard-Fusco, L. A. (2021, January 28). *Understanding Codependency.* Talkspace. https://www.talkspace.com/blog/codependency-what-is-definition/

Hughes, N. (2015, May 12). *It's Okay to Need a Little Help.* Tiny Buddha. https://tinybuddha.com/blog/its-okay-to-need-a-little-help/

Hutchinson, D. T. (2018, May 21). *Why are Personal Boundaries Important? Your Rights in a Relationship.* Tracy Hutchinson, PhD | Fort Myers Therapy. https://www.drtracyhutchinson.com/what-are-personal-boundaries-and-why-are-they-important/

IQ Matrix. (2015, March 3). *How to Build Self-Worth and Start Believing in Yourself Again.* IQ Matrix Blog. https://blog.iqmatrix.com/self-worth

Irwin, H. J. (1995). Codependence, narcissism, and childhood trauma. *Journal of Clinical Psychology, 51*(5), 658–665. Wiley Online Library. https://doi.org/3.0.CO;2-N10.1002/1097-4679(199509)51:5<658::aid-jclp2270510511>3.0.co;2-n">10.1002/1097-4679(199509)51:5<658::AID-JCLP2270510511>3.0.CO;2-N10.1002/1097-4679(199509)51:5<658::aid-jclp2270510511>3.0.co;2-n

James Madison University. (2022, June 27). *Counseling Center: Codependency.* Www.jmu.edu. https://www.jmu.edu/counselingctr/self-help/relationships/codependency.shtml

Johnson, E. B. (2019, September 23). *How to stop being a pushover and start being more assertive.* Practical Growth. https://medium.com/practical-growth/stop-being-a-pushover-7b4d7b199c85

Johnson, M. (n.d.). *Frequently asked questions: Unmasking Co-dependency.* Retrieved November 9, 2022, from https://www.mindfulinsight.co.za/pdf/Sacap+Codependency+talk+health.pdf

Keys. (2022, June 27). *How Hyper-Independence Will Ruin Your Dating Life.* Www.thekeys.ai. https://www.thekeys.ai/blog/how-hyper-independence-will-ruin-your-dating-life

Khazova, S. A., & Shipova, N. S. (2020). Emotional Intelligence as a Resource for Codependent Women. *European Proceedings of Social and Behavioural Sciences, 91*, 212–219. European Publisher. https://doi.org/10.15405/epsbs.2020.10.04.27

Killoren, C. (2021, July 16). *Codependency in Relationships: 10 Tips for Recognizing and Breaking the Cycle - Relish.* Hellorelish.com. https://hellorelish.com/articles/relationship-codependency-signs-tips.html

Lamm, B. (2018, January 4). *This is What Toxic Codependency Looks Like.* Breathe Life Healing - Addiction Treatment Center Los Angeles. https://breathelifehealingcenters.com/toxic-codependency-looks-like/

Lancer, D. (2013, September 29). *Transforming the Codependent Mind.* What Is Codependency? https://whatiscodependency.com/transforming-codependent-mind/

Lancer, D. (2015, March 1). *Breaking the Cycle of Abandonment*. What Is Codependency? https://whatiscodependency.com/breaking-the-cycle-of-abandonment/

Lancer, D. (2016, February 2). *Self-Esteem Makes or Breaks Relationships*. What Is Codependency? https://whatiscodependency.com/codependency-low-self-esteem-in-relationships/

Lancer, D. (2019a, April 3). *How to Leave a Narcissist or Toxic Relationship | Psychology Today*. Www.psychologytoday.com. https://www.psychologytoday.com/us/blog/toxic-relationships/201904/how-leave-narcissist-or-toxic-relationship?amp

Lancer, D. (2019b, July 23). *Narcissists Are Codependent, Too | Psychology Today*. Psychology Today. https://www.psychologytoday.com/us/blog/toxic-relationships/201907/narcissists-are-codependent-too?amp

Lancer, D. (2021, May 4). *Are Empaths Codependent?* What Is Codependency? https://whatiscodependency.com/are-empaths-codependent/

LePera, N. (2019, October 17). *Here's How To Tell The Difference Between Empathy & Codependency*. Mindbodygreen. https://www.mindbodygreen.com/articles/difference-between-empathy-and-codependent-behavior-for-hsps#:~:text=When%20another%20person%20is%20having

Lowrance, M. (2021, March 8). *6 Types of Boundaries & Questions to Explore Them*. Urban Wellness. https://urbanwellnesscounseling.com/6-types-of-boundaries/

Magee, H. (2019, August 4). *Codependency: More Than Just An Obsession With Our Lovers*. Medium. https://medium.com/@haileymagee/codependency-more-than-just-an-obsession-with-our-lovers-71e5eb2422f3

Magee, H. (2022, March 3). *How I Stopped Trying to Control My Partner and Took Responsibility for My Own Happiness*. Medium; Better Humans. https://betterhumans.pub/how-i-stopped-trying-to-control-my-partner-and-took-responsibility-for-my-own-happiness-da091ce799f5

Mairanz, A. (2019, October 10). *Turning off Self Judgment | Releasing Self Judgment by a NYC Therapist*. Empower Your Mind Therapy. https://eymtherapy.com/blog/self-judgment/

Manning-Schaffel, V. (2018, December 5). *What is codependency? Signs of a codependent relationship*. NBC News; NBC News. https://www.nbcnews.com/better/health/what-codependency-signs-codependent-relationship-ncna940666

Martin, S. (2017, July 28). *10 Things You Need to Know About Codependency*. Psych Central. https://psychcentral.com/blog/imperfect/2017/07/10-things-you-need-to-know-about-codependency#1

Martin, S. (2018a, April 24). *What are boundaries and why do I need them?* Live Well with Sharon Martin. https://www.livewellwithsharonmartin.com/what-are-boundaries/

Martin, S. (2018b, August 17). *Why Moving on from a Codependent Relationship Is so Difficult.* Psych Central. https://psychcentral.com/blog/imperfect/2018/08/why-moving-on-from-a-codependent-relationship-is-so-difficult

Martin, S. (2019, July 21). *Codependent Thinking: What It Is and How to Reframe It.* Sharon Martin, LCSW Counseling San Jose and Campbell, CA. https://sharonmartincounseling.com/codependent-thinking-san-jose-counseling/

Martin, S. (2020a, January 10). *Why Its So Hard to End a Codependent Relationship.* Psych Central. https://psychcentral.com/blog/imperfect/2020/01/why-its-so-hard-to-end-a-codependent-relationship

Martin, S. (2020b, April 23). *7 Types of Boundaries You May Need.* Psych Central. https://psychcentral.com/blog/imperfect/2020/04/7-types-of-boundaries-you-may-need

Martin, S. (2020c, June 7). *7 Reasons It's Hard to End Codependent Relationships.* Live Well with Sharon Martin. https://www.livewellwithsharonmartin.com/7-reasons-its-hard-to-end-codependent-relationships/

Martin, S. (2022, April 1). *Codependency and Boundaries.* Live Well with Sharon Martin. https://www.livewellwithsharonmartin.com/codependency-and-boundaries/

Matejko, S. (2022, August 24). *Help for Codependents Whose Relationships are Ending.* Psych Central. https://psychcentral.com/relationships/help-for-codependents-whose-relationships-are-ending

Mayfield, E. (2020, December 1). *Why do narcissists attract codependents? | Mindset Therapy*. www.mindsettherapyonline.com. https://www.mindsettherapyonline.com/blog/why-do-narcissists-attract-codependents

McLean, K. (2021, June 23). *Understanding Codependency (Anxious Attachment)*. Kennedymclean.com. https://www.kennedymclean.com/amp/understanding-codependency-anxious-attachment

Mental Health Center at Destination Hope. (2016, March 28). *Codependency: Your Questions Answered*. Mental Health Center. https://www.mentalhealthcenter.org/codependency-your-questions-answered/

Mightier. (2022, January 30). *What is Emotional Regulation?* Mightier. https://be.mightier.com/articles/what-is-emotional-regulation/

Mindy Fox, LMFT. (2019, April 30). *How Codependency And Low Self Esteem Go Together* -. Mindy Fox, MFT Neurofeedback Los Angeles, Santa Monica and Torrance CA. https://mftherapy.com/dating-tips/how-codependency-and-low-self-esteem-go-together/

Moore, M. (2021, November 11). *Narcissist and Codependent Compatibility in Relationships*. Psych Central. https://psychcentral.com/disorders/the-dance-between-codependents-narcissists

Moore, M. (2022, September 8). *Here's 3 Ways Boundaries Can Help You*. Psych Central. https://psychcentral.com/relationships/the-importance-of-personal-boundaries

Morin, A. (2019). *5 ways to start boosting your self-confidence today.* Verywell Mind. https://www.verywellmind.com/how-to-boost-your-self-confidence-4163098

Mullins, R. (2019, November 30). *Codependency and Enablers: Understanding and Changing the Relationship Dynamics.* Rachel Mullins Counseling. https://rachelmullinscounseling.com/2019/11/30/codependency-and-enablers-understanding-and-changing-the-relationship-dynamics/amp/

My AttachEd. (2021, December 10). *Codependency in Anxious Attachment & Fearful Avoidant Attachment: How to Stop Being Codependent.* My AttachEd. https://myattached.com/2021/12/09/codependency-in-anxious-attachment-fearful-avoidant-attachment-how-to-stop-being-codependent/?amp=1

Newport Academy. (2012, March 4). *Codependency Disorder - Codependency & Relationships.* Newport Academy. https://www.newportacademy.com/resources/restoring-families/codependency-disorder/

Nguyen, J. (2020, October 20). *Codependent vs. Interdependent Relationships: How To Spot The Difference.* Mindbodygreen. https://www.mindbodygreen.com/articles/codependency-vs-interdependency

NHS. (2021, February 1). *Raising low self-esteem.* Nhs.uk. https://www.nhs.uk/mental-health/self-help/tips-and-support/raise-low-self-esteem/

Northwestern Medicine Staff. (2017, February 13). *5 Benefits of Healthy Relationships*. Northwestern Medicine. https://www.nm.org/healthbeat/healthy-tips/5-benefits-of-healthy-relationships

Pace, R. (2021, August 6). *How to Stop Being Toxic in a Relationship*. Marriage Advice - Expert Marriage Tips & Advice. https://www.marriage.com/advice/relationship/how-to-stop-being-toxic-in-a-relationship/

Pattemore, C. (2021, June 3). *10 Ways to Build and Preserve Better Boundaries*. Psych Central. https://psychcentral.com/lib/10-way-to-build-and-preserve-better-boundaries

Perth Counselling And Psychotherapy. (2021, July 20). *Signs You're In A Codependent or Interdependent Relationship*. Perth Counselling and Psychotherapy. https://perthcounsellingandpsychotherapy.com.au/signs-youre-in-a-codependent-or-interdependent-relationship/#:~:text=While%20codependency%20is%20an%20unequal

Pietrangelo, A. (2019, February 13). *What Is Fear of Abandonment, and Can It Be Treated?* Healthline; Healthline Media. https://www.healthline.com/health/fear-of-abandonment

Power of Positivity. (2020, March 13). *Psychology Explains When Codependency Turns Unhealthy*. Power of Positivity: Positive Thinking & Attitude. https://www.powerofpositivity.com/codependency-turns-unhealthy-psychology-explains/?amp

Rainey, Dr. R. (2019, July 18). *Codependency: What Is It? - Focus on the Family*. Focus on the Family. https://www.focusonthefamily.com/get-help/codependency-what-is-it/

Reachout. (n.d.). *How to build self-confidence*. Au.reachout.com. https://au.reachout.com/articles/how-to-build-self-confidence

Rebecca. (2022, June). *Importance and Strategies on Emotion Regulation*. Heal Autism Centre. https://www.healisautism.com/amp/importance-strategies-emotion-regulation

Rediscovering Sacredness. (2019, January 22). *Please Don't Leave Me! The Fear Of Abandonment*. Rediscovering Sacredness | Dominica Applegate. https://rediscoveringsacredness.com/the-fear-of-abandonment/

Rembold, T. (2021, August 19). *7 Common Roles in a Dysfunctional Family. | elephant journal*. Elephant Journal | Daily Blog, Videos, E-Newsletter & Magazine on Yoga + Organics + Green Living + Non-New Agey Spirituality + Ecofashion + Conscious Consumerism=It's about the Mindful Life. https://www.elephantjournal.com/2021/08/dysfunctional-family-dynamics/

Rosenberg, R. (2014, March 12). *The dance between codependents and narcissists*. Counseling Today. https://ct.counseling.org/2014/03/the-dance-between-codependents-and-narcissists/

Rosenberg, R. (2016, January 17). *Empaths vs. Codependents*. Psych Central. https://psychcentral.com/blog/empaths-vs-codependents#1

Sana Counselling. (2022, June 6). *When People Pleasing is a Trauma Response: Fawn Trauma Explained.* Sana Counselling. https://sanacounselling.ca/blog/when-people-pleasing-is-a-trauma-response-fawn-trauma

Santilli, M., Howard, M., & Migala, J. (2022, March 1). *You May Be In A Codependent Relationship If Your Fights Feel Super Repetitive.* Women's Health. https://www.womenshealthmag.com/relationships/a19596563/codependent-relationship-signs/

Saviuc, L. D. (2020, August 18). *5 Healthy Ways to Let go of Self Judgment - Purpose Fairy.* Www.purposefairy.com. https://www.purposefairy.com/91758/let-go-self-judgment/

Schmidt, B. (2022, January 6). *How To Heal From A Codependent Relationship When It Ends.* Bolde. https://www.bolde.com/how-to-heal-from-a-codependent-relationship-when-it-ends/

SCL Health. (2019, September). *How to Cultivate Healthy Relationships and Avoid Toxic Ones.* Www.sclhealth.org. https://www.sclhealth.org/blog/2019/09/how-to-cultivate-healthy-relationships-and-avoid-toxic-ones/

Seasons in Malibu, & nationalpositions Primary Therapist. (2018, March 21). *Does Lack of Self Worth Make you Co-Dependent?* Luxury Rehab for Addiction and Mental Health Treatment | Seasons in Malibu. https://seasonsmalibu.com/does-lack-of-self-worth-make-you-co-dependent/#:~:text=A%20codependent%20person%20may%20have

Selva, J. (2018, February 9). *Codependency: What Are The Signs & How To Overcome It.* PositivePsychology.com. https://positivepsychology.com/codependency-definition-signs-worksheets/

Sinclair, L. (2021, December 29). *Mental health: Why being too independent can be a bad thing.* Stylist. https://www.stylist.co.uk/health/mental-health/hyper-independence-tiktok-signs-experts/606443

SkillsYouNeed. (2011). *Improving Self-Esteem | Skills You Need.* Skillsyouneed.com. https://www.skillsyouneed.com/ps/self-esteem.html

Smith, K. (2022, May 20). *Signs of a Codependent vs. Interdependent Relationship.* Psych Central. https://psychcentral.com/lib/codependency-vs-interdependency

Soghomonian, I. (2019, September 23). *Boundaries - Why are they important? Part 1.* The Resilience Centre. https://www.theresiliencecentre.com.au/boundaries-why-are-they-important/#:~:text=Why%20Are%20Boundaries%20Important%3F

Steber, C. (2019, August 1). *How To Prevent Toxicity In Your Relationship, According To Experts.* Bustle. https://www.bustle.com/p/how-to-prevent-toxicity-in-your-relationship-according-to-experts-18494180

Sunshine Behavioral Health. (2019, July 3). *Fear Abandonment Codependency - Sunshine Behavioral Health.* Sunshine Behavioral Health. https://www.sunshinebehavioralhealth.com/blog/fear-abandonment-codependency/#:~:text=The%20fear%20of%20abandonment%20is

Svoboda, M. (2021, June 3). *Givers have to set limits because takers rarely do.* Quotepark.com. https://quotepark.com/quotes/1085682-henry-ford-givers-have-to-set-limits-because-takers-rarely-do/

T. C. M. World. (2020, May 5). *Give, But Only From Your Overflow.* TCM World. https://www.tcmworld.org/give-but-only-from-your-overflow/

TD Jakes. (2022). *3 Reasons It's OK To Ask For Help.* TDJakes.com. https://www.tdjakes.com/posts/3-reasons-it-s-ok-to-ask-for-help

Team Tony. (2021, July 30). *5 ways to start prioritizing yourself today | Tony Robbins.* Tony Robbins. https://www.tonyrobbins.com /mind-meaning/how-to-prioritize-yourself/

Telloian, C. (2021, November 5). *4 Tips to Overcome Fear of Abandonment.* Psych Central. https://psychcentral.com/health/fear-of-abandonment

University of Illinois Chicago. (2022, February 25). *Boundaries: What are they and how to create them | Wellness Center | University of Illinois Chicago.* Wellnesscenter.uic.edu. https://wellnesscenter.uic.edu/news-stories/boundaries-what-are-they-and-how-to-create-them/

Villines, Z. (2018, August 7). *Codependency and Narcissism May Have More in Common Than You Think - GoodTherapy.org Therapy Blog.* Good Therapy. https://www.goodtherapy.org/blog/codependency-narcissism-may-have-more-in-common-than-you-think-0807187/amp/

Walsh, Dr. W. (2015, October 12). *4 Ways to Avoid Toxic Relationships Altogether*. ELLE. https://www.elle.com/life-love/sex-relationships/a31121/4-ways-to-avoid-a-toxic-relationship/

Washington, J. (2019, June 26). *How Empty and Dry is Your Well?* WHAT NOW? LIFE COACHING. https://www.whatnowlifecoaching.com/mushroom-to-sunflower-blo/how-empty-and-dry-is-your-well

Whitener, S. (2020, August 6). *Council Post: How To Develop Self-Reliance And Overcome Codependency*. Forbes. https://www.forbes.com/sites/forbescoachescouncil/2020/08/06/how-to-develop-self-reliance-and-overcome-codependency/?sh=6b9d0e076955

Wikipedia. (2022, May 5). *Emotional self-regulation*. Wikipedia. https://en.m.wikipedia.org/wiki/Emotional_self-regulation

Yuko, E. (2022, September 13). *This Is What It Looks Like to Set Personal and Emotional Boundaries*. Real Simple. https://www.realsimple.com/health/mind-mood/emotional-health/how-to-set-boundaries

Made in the USA
Las Vegas, NV
05 December 2023